Timeless Recipes

featuring Tasty Singapore food products

Contents

Foreword

A good recipe is usually one that is tried and tested over many years. It is a tradition that, once perfected, is always generously shared and even passed down through generations, to ensure that as many people as possible savour its delectable flavour and delicious taste.

In developing this unique **'Timeless Recipes'** cookbook, the International Enterprise Singapore (IE Singapore) shares time-tested favourite local recipes through this sampler book featuring easy-to-cook menu ideas perfectly suited for any occasion, any season. Co-developed with Singapore's prominent culinary icon, Violet Oon, this book provides many recipe ideas, from appetisers and main courses, to desserts and drinks, each one showing how easily and quickly authentic local favourite dishes can be prepared using locally-manufactured products bearing the Tasty Singapore mark.

IE Singapore plays a major role in helping local food manufacturers internationalise their products under its Tasty Singapore brand. In showcasing the convenience and simplicity of using Tasty Singapore products to prepare these delicious recipes, and leveraging the high quality standards that Singapore is internationally renowned for, IE Singapore hopes to encourage more people to trust and rely on the Tasty Singapore brand to prepare their favourite Singapore food, wherever in the world they may be.

Within these pages, one will find several ways to prepare their favourite Singapore dishes using Tasty Singapore products. In addition, the book features innovative ways to adapt these products for other creative cooking ideas. Ultimately, these Tasty Singapore recipes represent the passion, confidence, distinctiveness and East-West fusion that goes into preparing Singapore food, an experience that Singapore would like to share with the rest of the world.

Chong Lit Cheong
Chief Executive Officer
International Enterprise Singapore

Tasty Singapore

Singapore has long envisioned building itself a world-class identity to characterise its culinary passion and capabilities for food production. Indeed, the country is already universally acknowledged as a food paradise and, in line with increasing globalisation in food manufacturing and retailing, has developed a strong core positioning, that of 'Tasty Singapore', which has effectively captured the traits, culture and personality of Singapore food manufacturing under one unique yet unified identity.

Developed as a collaborative effort between IE Singapore, the Singapore Food Manufacturers' Association and the Singapore Manufacturers' Federation, and supported by SPRING Singapore, the 'Tasty Singapore' identity encapsulates the distinctive personality and flavours of Singapore food yet also emphasises a global benchmark in creativity, innovativeness, technology, quality and tradition in preparing products carrying this branding. Distinguished by an easily recognised logo, the brand itself is associated with high value and represents the essence of Singapore food, reflecting the variety, taste and high standards that are incorporated into its food production methods.

As an encompassing brand itself, 'Tasty Singapore' promises four key attributes – that of Confidence, a strong self assurance in the inherent high manufacturing standards of its products; Passion, a fervour in harnessing the emotive delight in Singapore's delicious food varieties; Distinctiveness, the unique edge in its manufacturing processes, packaging design and nutritional values; and East-West Fusion, the harnessing of the best of all worlds in terms of cultures, styles and tastes.

The Tasty Singapore Brand Ambassadors – qualified Singapore food manufacturing companies with products bearing the 'Tasty Singapore' mark – represent world-class competencies in terms of reliability and consistency of taste and flavours, excellence in quality and safety standards as well as efficiency in supply chain management. Together with quality ingredients and the promise of an authentic Singaporean experience, the 'Tasty Singapore' marque now commands global recognition and an international competitiveness that has ensured Singapore's solid standing on the world stage for culinary excellence.

Singapore Food
— a reflection of its history

Singaporeans have a special love affair with the island's cuisine; its unique flavour, tempting aromas, visual impact and even preparation sounds distinguish Singapore food from the other cuisines of the world.

Singaporeans love their food and within every Singaporean is a sophisticated gourmet. Regardless of status and profession, they can talk passionately, in-depth and at great length, about the colourful dishes that make up the Singapore culinary landscape, especially about their particular favourite dish.

This landscape has developed and evolved through the years. Today it continues to change and grow, with new and innovative dishes being introduced constantly.

While a wide array of dining styles can be found in Singapore, Singaporeans love their 'hawker centres', a common feature in every residential estate. At these centres, a variety of 'street food' from the different local ethnic groups can be found. They not only taste splendid but are also a perfect chronicle of the history of early immigrants to Singapore who came here to make a living.

In 1819, Sir Stamford Raffles of the British East India Company arrived in Singapore and saw great potential in the island to be an important

View of Clarke Quay from Kyomomoyama Restaurant

'Flipping' dough to fine, crispy Roti Prata

Food Republic, the modern hawker centre

port of call to bridge the East and the West. The establishment of Singapore attracted mainly immigrants from China, India and the Malay Peninsula; Chinese, Indians and Malays would eventually make up the three main ethnic groups of modern Singapore.

Many early immigrants were men who came to Singapore on their own, leaving their families behind. Cooking was not a priority and many depended on street food vendors who would visit work sites to sell their food. This was simple fare, readily available and cheap. Subsequently, more formal establishments were set up where these vendors had a more permanent place to sell their food offerings. Thus, the hawker centre was born.

Hawker cuisine today reflects the ethnic character and personality of Singapore. This cuisine is a unique blend of the many eastern cultures present here: the Southern Chinese, mainly the Hokkien, Teochew, Cantonese and Hainanese; the South Indians from Kerala and South India Indian Muslims, as well as the native cuisine of the Malay Peninsula, which include elements from both ethnic Malay as well as Straits Chinese influences.

The Singapore cuisine brings together the cooking traditions of all these settlers. Indian cooking relies on dried seeds and hard spices like coriander, cumin, fennel, fenugreek, cloves, cinnamon, and cardamom. The Malays use mainly fresh root spices, herbs and fresh aromatic fruit skins such galangal, lemongrass, turmeric, basil leaves and coriander roots. The Chinese were concerned with the 'ying and yang' of cooking, using herbs and other ingredients to provide health and balance to the body and its overall well-being.

As Singapore grew and prospered, the immigrants made the island state their home. The inter-racial interactions gave rise to a uniquely Singapore cuisine that reflected the influence that the different cultures had on one

Old world hawker charm at Food Republic

The outdoor pool bar at Café Del Mar, Sentosa

Simple elegance at Whitebait and Kale

another. This cuisine was found at hawker centres as well as in some of the more upscale restaurants that emerged in the 1950s and 1960s.

In recent years, Singapore's food manufacturers have captured and transformed many of these beloved traditional dishes into conveniently prepared home cooking. A wide array of food items were introduced, from dishes that only required heating, to premixes, sauces and instant beverage mixes. These not only apply to home-prepared meals but are also used in the food services industry. Tasty Singapore's **'Timeless Recipes'** showcase a selection of these well-loved dishes cooked in their traditional way as well as in a convenient-style.

'Timeless Recipes' offers a modern twist to old time favourites. In the fast paced modern Singapore society, the temptation of dining out is great. These quick and easy-to-cook recipes will provide solutions for delicious and easy-to-prepare home cooked meals.

Sun, sea and sand at Café del Mar, Sentosa

Short days, long nights and the biting cold of winter are turning into days of gentler clime and sunlit afternoons. The promise of life is in the earth, with new shoots emerging from the soil. It's a time to enjoy lighter foods and crisper flavours.

Spring...

Kung Po is a dish special to the Sichuan province in China where the region's fiery dried red chilli peppers make their presence felt in a recipe that is spicy hot, sweet and sour. Cashew nuts add that special crunchy bite to this dish of layered textures and flavours.

Squid with Roasted Cashews in Kung Po Sauce

Preparation time: 15 minutes   Cooking time: 5 minutes   To serve: 4

6 tbsp SUNBEAM corn oil • 100g each of red, green & yellow Capsicum • 100g cut onions • 4 slices ginger • 20g spring onions, cut into 1cm lengths • 8 dried chillies, cut into 2cm lengths • 200g squid or chicken cut in cubes • 120g **CAMEL Salted Cashews** • ¹/₂ bottle (120ml) CHNG KEE'S Kung Po Sauce

Heat 3 tablespoons oil, add capsicum and onions, stir fry over high heat for 1 minute, and remove from heat. Add remaining oil, ginger, spring onions and chillies and stir fry over high heat till fragrant. Stir in squid and cook for 2 minutes. Add **CAMEL Salted Cashews**. Fry briefly, add Kung Po Sauce, mix well for 10 seconds. Serve with steamed rice or on its own.

Food notes: CAMEL Salted Cashews come in packets of 40g and 180g.

Where available: CAMEL products can be found in Asia, Europe, the Middle East and the USA.

traditional kung po sauce

Preparation time: 5 minutes   Cooking time: Nil   To serve: 2 - 3

Ingredients: 1 tbsp dark soya sauce • 1 tbsp Chinese yellow wine or dry sherry • 1¹/₂ tsp rice vinegar or red wine vinegar • 1¹/₂ tsp fine sugar • 1 tsp sesame oil • 1 tsp corn flour • 1 tbsp water

Method: Mix all the ingredients together and use in place of the Kung Po Sauce in the recipe for Squid with Roasted Cashews in Kung Po Sauce.

Capsicums

new ideas

CAMEL Salted Cashews are fried to crisp perfection and taste delicious as a snack. They can be used in main dishes as well as in desserts and cookies. Brush off the salt and crush into small pieces to accompany vanilla ice cream served with caramel sauce for a great dessert. For cookies, grind **CAMEL Salted Cashews** to a rough texture and add to cookie dough before baking. You will find the aroma and flavour of the cookies alluringly delicious.

home-made tofu

Tofu preparation time: 30 minutes   Pressing time: 20 - 30 minutes

Ingredients: 1 portion of soya bean milk made from 250g dried soya beans (see recipe for Mango Pudding for making soya bean milk) • 1 tsp Epsom salts (Magnesium Sulphate) • 1 large piece of cheese cloth or muslin measuring 50cm by 50cm square • 1 sieve • a pestle and mortar or a heavy weight • 1 large bowl

Method: Heat soya bean milk to 75 degrees Celsius. Add Epsom salts, stir well. The curds (the solid bits) and whey (the liquid) will separate. Leave for 30 minutes, then pour into a sieve lined with muslin and placed over a bowl. Twist the cloth to squeeze out the excess whey and place a heavy weight on top for 30 minutes to form a firm tofu. Remove from muslin.

Tofu

new ideas

UNICURD Tofu can be cut into cubes and deep fried or lightly oiled and baked in the oven. It provides the much needed protein in vegetarian diets. Tofu cubes can be mixed into salads like Waldorf, Cobb or Russian salads.

Tofu Croquettes

Preparation time: 30 minutes   Cooking time: 15 minutes   To serve: 4

300g **UNICURD Pressed Tofu** • 40g shallots or onions, finely chopped • 50g (2 numbers) water chestnuts, peeled and diced finely • 10g spring onions, finely chopped • 15g (2 numbers) Shitake mushrooms • 1/2 egg white • 1/2 - 3/4 tsp salt • 50g fresh corn kernel • 1/8 tsp white pepper powder • 1/8 tsp sesame oil • 2 - 3 tbsp plain flour • 100g prawn meat, optional • 2 litres of SUNBEAM sunflower oil

Place mashed **UNICURD Pressed Tofu** on a piece of muslin cloth, squeeze out the liquid and place in a sieve. Press a heavy weight on top and leave the weight there for 15 minutes to remove excess water. Remove mashed tofu and mix the tofu with the rest of the ingredients except the oil. Make patties of about 30g each and deep fry in SUNBEAM sunflower oil till golden brown. Serve with Mayo Honey Sauce.

Mayo Honey Sauce: Mix 1/2 tbsp of mayonnaise with 1 tbsp of honey and a pinch of salt.

Food notes: UNICURD makes a variety of tofu and hard tofu products (tau kwa). The silken tofu is ideal for steaming and for soups while the pressed homemade tofu is of a firmer texture and contains less water. UNICURD silken tofu comes in 300g packets and needs to be kept chilled.

Where available: UNICURD food products can be found in Asia, Europe and the USA.

Tofu is known as the meat of Asia as this smooth as silk soya bean product is rich in vegetable protein.

Poached Beef Rolls with Sauce Hainanese

Preparation time: 20 minutes	Cooking time: 3 minutes	To serve: 4

300g fillet of beef cut from the thick end • 50g carrots, peeled and cut into finger length julienne • 50g cucumber, cut into finger length julienne • 50g Enoki mushrooms, cut into finger lengths, discard the roots • 1 packet **MY MUM'S Sauce for Singapore Hainanese Beef Noodle**

Slice the beef along the long side of the fillet, thinly and into 2. On each slice of beef place a piece each of carrot, cucumber and Enoki mushrooms and roll tightly. Boil about 3 cups water in a frying pan over high heat. Lower the flame so water comes to a rolling boil. Put the beef rolls in the water. Lightly poach the rolls till the beef changes colour – this takes about 4 to 5 seconds. Remove the rolls with a pair of tongs or chopsticks and put on a tray lined with paper towels. Put the whole pouch of **MY MUM'S Sauce for Singapore Hainanese Beef Noodle** in a pot of boiling water for 3 to 4 minutes. Remove. Cut open the pouch and pour sauce over the beef rolls. Serve.

Food notes: MY MUM'S Sauce for Singapore Hainanese Beef Noodle comes in sterilised foil packets of 150g each. No MSG or preservatives are used.

Where available: MY MUM'S products can be found in Europe, the Middle East and the USA.

traditional hainanese beef sauce

Preparation time: 15 minutes	Cooking time: 3 hours	To serve: 4

Ingredients: 2 litres water • 2 tbsp cornflour (cornstarch) • 500g shin beef, cut into 3cm cubes • 6 dried cloves • 2 cinnamon sticks measuring 5cm each • 2 whole star anise • 5 cloves garlic, peeled and smashed lightly to break open • 5 peeled shallots • 3 tsp dark soya sauce

Method: Mix 3 tablespoons of water with cornflour and keep aside. Mix the remaining water with the rest of the ingredients and bring to boil on high heat. Lower the heat and simmer for 3 hours till the soup stock is aromatic. Strain the stock and discard the spices, beef, garlic and shallots. There should be about 300ml of stock. Bring the stock to a boil and mix in the cornflour mixture, stirring constantly till the sauce thickens.

Enoki mushrooms

*The fragrant spices of cloves,
cinnamon and star anise add a great
flavour to a traditional beef sauce.*

*new
ideas*

Serving **MY MUM'S Sauce for
Singapore Hainanese Beef Noodle**
over delicate beef rolls is a novel interpretation
of an old-world village favourite.

Roast meats are so central to the Cantonese culinary tradition that there is a separate roast meat kitchen in Cantonese restaurants. Char Siew is one of the most popular roast meats.

Chinese Barbeque Lamb with Char Siew Sauce

Preparation time: 15 minutes   Marinating time: 4 - 8 hours
Cooking time: 10 - 20 minutes   To serve: 4

1kg of rack of lamb, cut into 4 portions (about 4 ribs per portion) • 1 bottle **CHNG KEE'S Asian Originals Char Siew Sauce** • 2 tbsp SUNBEAM corn oil or olive oil

Wash lamb and pat dry with paper towels. Marinate with **CHNG KEE'S Asian Originals Char Siew Sauce**, place in container, cover and store in the chiller for at least 4 to 8 hours or more. Pre-heat oven to 200 degrees Celsius for 10 minutes. Put the lamb on a baking tray lined with foil. Heat oil and pour over the lamb pieces. Put the baking tray on the top or higher shelf of the oven and roast/grill for 10 to 20 minutes till the lamb is brown and crisp. Turn heat down to 180 degrees Celsius to further cook the lamb if you find it too rare. The lamb should be pink on the bone. If this is the first time you are roasting lamb, test for doneness by cutting into the centre of the rack. If it is too pink and rare, put the tray back into the oven to roast for 3 to 4 more minutes till the meat is done the way you like. Serve with steamed and buttered carrots and a selection of vegetables.

Food notes: CHNG KEE'S Asian Originals Char Siew Sauce comes in bottles of 240ml (250g) nett or in catering packs of 1kg or more.

Where available: CHNG KEE'S Asian Originals and other Sin Hwa Dee products can be found in Asia, Europe and the Middle East.

traditional char siew marinade

Preparation time: 20 minutes   Cooking time: Nil   To serve: 4

Ingredients: 3 cloves garlic • $^{1}/_{2}$ - 1 tsp five-spice powder (to taste)
• 3 tbsp light soya sauce • 1 tbsp black bean paste or brown bean paste
• 2 tbsp hoi sin sauce • 2 tbsp Chinese yellow wine or dry sherry, optional
• 2 tbsp tomato ketchup • 1 tsp sesame oil • 2 tbsp fine sugar • 1 tbsp honey

Method: Peel and finely chop the garlic. Mix all the ingredients and use as a marinade for meat.

Cloves

new ideas **CHNG KEE'S Asian Originals Char Siew Sauce** can be served as a sauce on its own to accompany roast or fried meats.

traditional singapore home style laksa gravy

Preparation time: 40 minutes   Cooking time: 20 minutes   To serve: 4 - 6

Ingredients for gravy: 50g Galangal (Lengkuas) • 2 stalks lemon grass (Serai) • 3 candlenuts (Buah Keras) • 1cm length Tumeric (Kunyit), peeled • 15 dried chillies, remove seeds and soak in hot water • 3 cloves garlic, peeled • 2 tsp shrimp paste (Belachan) • 100g shallots, peeled • 1 tsp white pepper powder • 1½ tbsp coriander powder (Ketumbar) •30g dried prawns • 2 - 3 cups of water • 3 cups chilled coconut milk or pasteurised coconut cream • 1 - 1½ tsp salt • 4 to 6 tbsp vegetable oil

Method: Peel Galangal. Slice lemon grass, 2cm from the base/root. Grind the first 8 ingredients with pepper till fine. Heat oil over high heat, add ground spices and dried prawns and fry for 8 minutes till fragrant. Add coriander, water and half of the coconut milk, bring to boil and then simmer for 15 minutes. Add remaining coconut milk and salt and bring to boil again, stirring constantly.

Laksa

Preparation time: 25 minutes   Cooking time: 15 minutes   To serve: 2 - 3

1 box **PRIMA TASTE Ready-to-Cook Meal Kit for Laksa** • 600ml water • 300g fresh thick rice vermicelli or 150g PEACOCK BRAND dried rice spaghetti • 1 handful fresh bean sprouts, roots removed, lightly blanched and drained • 150g prawns, steamed and peeled • 80g cucumber, cut into fine julienne or into long thin slices • 6 hard-boiled quail's eggs or 1 hard boiled chicken egg • 1 deep fried soya bean cake (tau pok), optional • 200g fresh cockles, optional • 2 fresh laksa leaves, optional

Put Laksa pre-mix from the **PRIMA TASTE Ready-to-Cook Meal Kit for Laksa** into a small saucepan; add 600ml water and the Laksa paste. Mix well till all the ingredients are dissolved, bring to boil on high heat. Stir well, add dried laksa leaves and simmer for 2 to 3 minutes. This makes about 3½ cups of gravy. Turn off heat. Keep pan covered. Cook PEACOCK BRAND dried rice spaghetti in a big pot of boiling water for 2 to 3 minutes till the rice spaghetti is soft. Drain and blanch in cold water. If you are using fresh thick rice vermicelli, pour boiling water on the vermicelli, mix well and drain. Put the spaghetti into 2 or 3 bowls, add bean sprouts, and pour in the Laksa gravy. Add prawns, cucumber, eggs, sliced fried soya bean cake and lightly poached cockles. Garnish with julienne of fresh Laksa leaves. Serve sambal chilli on a side plate and add extra chilli to taste.

Food notes: Each box of **PRIMA TASTE Ready-to-Cook Meal Kit for Laksa** weighs 225g and contains 1 foil sachet each of Laksa paste (containing spice paste), Laksa pre-mix (containing coconut), sambal chilli and dried Laksa leaves (polygonum hydropiper).

Where available: PRIMA Food products can be found in Asia, Australia, Canada, the USA and the UK.

In Singapore, it is a hotly contested decision as to which food stall serves the best and most authentic Laksa as we are so fond of this dish and its traditional taste.

new ideas

Laksa Gravy is a delicious spiced broth and can be served in many ways. Lobster with Laksa Sauce is a great idea. Poach halved lobster, lightly blanch some zucchini and add rich thick Laksa Gravy. Using the **PRIMA TASTE Ready-to-Cook Meal Kit for Laksa**, add 400ml water instead of 600ml to create a thick rich sauce.

Fish Tempra

TASTY
Singapore

Preparation time: 15 minutes   Cooking time: 20 minutes   To serve: 4

200g fresh red chillies, stalks removed • 500g onions, peeled • ³/₄ cup vegetable oil • ¹/₂ - ³/₄ cup **ONG'S Sweet Indonesian Soy Sauce** • juice of 10 small limes (Calamansi in Filipino and Limau Kesturi in Malay) or 2 lemons • 150g fillet of sea bass per person x 4

Slice chillies and onions. Pour ¹/₂ cup vegetable oil into heated wok and add onions, stir fry for 1 minute before adding chillies. Stir fry till fragrant. Remove ¹/₄ for the garnish. Continue to stir fry onions and chillies for 2 to 3 minutes till soft. Add **ONG'S Sweet Indonesian Soy Sauce** and simmer gently for 2 minutes over medium heat. Add lime or lemon juice to make a sweet and sour sauce. Put aside. Heat a frying pan, add the remaining oil and pan fry the fish fillet in hot oil on each side for 3 to 4 minutes till golden brown. Serve the Fish Tempra on a bed of greens with the sauce. Garnish with onions and chillies.

Food notes: ONG'S Sweet Indonesian Soy Sauce, sold in 430ml bottles, is called Ketchup Manis in Indonesian and is soya sauce with sugar. Tempra sauce is usually made with dark soy sauce and sugar. ONG'S sauce makes the dish simpler to cook.

Where available: ONG'S and other Bachun Food products can be found in the Asia Pacific, Africa, Europe and the USA.

chicken tempra original

Preparation time: 20 minutes   Cooking time: 35 - 40 minutes   Serves: 4 - 6

Ingredients: ³/₄ cup dark soya sauce • 1kg chicken, cut into large pieces, bones included • 200g fresh red chillies, stalks removed, sliced • 500g onions, peeled and cut into rings • ¹/₂ cup vegetable oil • 5 - 6 tbsp sugar • ¹/₄ cup water • juice of 10 small limes

Method: Marinate the chicken with 2 tablespoons soya sauce for 10 minutes. Add ¹/₂ cup vegetable oil to hot wok and stir fry onions and chillies for 4 to 5 minutes. Remove ¹/₄ for the garnish. Add chicken to the wok, and stir fry for 4 minutes, add remaining soya sauce, sugar and water and boil for 35 to 40 minutes till chicken is tender. Add lime juice, stir well.

Fresh red chillies

new ideas

Traditionally, Chicken Tempra is a hearty, delicious, sweet and sour stew. Cooking fish with **ONG'S Sweet Indonesian Soy Sauce** and serving the dish on a bed of greens is a new style which can translate well into the menus of any international kitchen. Al dente spaghetti makes the perfect accompaniment to the delicious sauce.

Tempra is a unique recipe from Singapore's Peranakan cuisine, a hybrid of Chinese and Malay cooking.

traditional cereal with yoghurt and berries

Preparation time: 10 minutes   Cooking time: Nil   To serve: 1

Ingredients: 1 sachet instant cereal • 2 tbsp hot water • 1 tbsp raisins • 3 - 4 tbsp natural plain yoghurt • 3 strawberries, cut into quarters • 5 blueberries • 5 raspberries

Method: Mix instant cereal with hot water and add raisins. Leave for 5 minutes for cereal to plump up. Put in a tall wine glass. Top with unsweetened yoghurt and add berries. Chill and serve as a refreshing breakfast or a mid morning snack.

Assorted berries

new ideas

Dip peeled bananas into milk or beaten eggs and coat with **SUPER Instant Nutritious Cereal**. Leave for 2 to 3 minutes for the cereal to adhere to the bananas. Fry in hot oil till crispy and brown.

Super Coffee Cookies with Cereal

Preparation time: 20 minutes   Baking time: 10 - 15 minutes   To serve: 10 - 12

200g (1¾ cup) plain flour • 125g butter, softened at room temperature • 1 egg • ½ tsp vanilla essence • 4 sachets **SUPER Instant Nutritious Cereal** • 1 sachet SUPER COFFEEMIX 3-in-1 coffee

Mix flour with butter, egg and vanilla essence. Add contents of 3 sachets of **SUPER Instant Nutritious Cereal** and mix well into biscuit (cookie) dough. Divide the dough into 2 equal parts and mix one part with SUPER COFFEEMIX 3-in-1 coffee. Form both parts of dough into fingers and sprinkle additional **SUPER Instant Nutritious Cereal** on top. Create the pattern by using the thin ends of 2 chopsticks to press down on each cookie. Pre-heat the oven at 180 degrees Celsius for 10 minutes. Bake for 10 to 15 minutes till cookies are cooked, crisp and fragrant. Serve with a cup of coffee for a delicious dessert or as a snack.

Food notes: SUPER COFFEEMIX 3-in-1 coffee (20g per sachet and 48 sachets per pack) contains coffee, sugar and creamer. The **SUPER Instant Nutritious Cereal** contains whole wheat, rice and maize as well as sugar and creamer in 30g sachets, and makes for an instant breakfast cereal treat when mixed with 1 cup hot water. There are 20 sachets per packet.

Where available: SUPER Instant Nutritious Cereal and other SUPER products can be found in Asia, Europe, the Middle East and the USA.

Cookies with cereal are very popular in Singapore and are usually served at open houses during festive seasons like Chinese New Year, the Indian Deepavali Festival of Lights and the Malay Eid celebrations.

*Spring Rolls are a staple in Chinese
cuisine and are usually filled with a
savoury vegetable stew and deep fried. Our
Spring Roll debuts as a dessert and is
oven baked for a crisp effect.*

Spring Rolls with a Fruit Medley

Preparation time: 30 minutes   Cooking time: 20 minutes   To serve: 3

9 **SPRING HOME TYJ Spring Roll Pastry** sheets • 100g raisins • 80g seedless dates • 2 tbsp lemon juice • 3 tbsp water • 30g brown sugar (2 tbsp) • ½ tsp vanilla essence • 100g melted butter • 2 tsp finely grated orange peel • 2½ tbsp Orange Sauce by ONG'S • flesh of 1 orange, cut into cubes • ½ tsp of cornflour mixed with 1 tbsp water

Defrost 1 packet of **SPRING HOME TYJ Spring Roll Pastry** sheets for 20 minutes. For filling, put raisins, dates, lemon juice, water, brown sugar and vanilla in a small saucepan and stir for 1 minute till the mixture is well mixed. Spread out spring roll skin, brush with melted butter, put 1 tablespoon of filling in the centre and fold into a spring roll. Bake in preheated oven at 180 degrees Celsius for 10 minutes till golden brown and the spring roll skin is crispy. Put the remaining ingredients in a small saucepan and stir on high heat for 1 minute till it thickens. Serve with the Spring Rolls.

Food notes: SPRING HOME TYJ Spring Roll Pastry by Tee Yih Jia comes in packets of 40 sheets measuring 215mm x 215mm and weighs a total of 550g. Smaller spring roll sheets are also available. The skins should be stored at -18 degrees Celsius.

Where available: SPRING HOME and other Tee Yih Jia products can be found in Asia, Canada, the Middle East, the USA and the UK.

mum's spring rolls

Preparation time: 1 hour   Cooking time: 30 minutes   To serve: 10

Ingredients: 20 spring roll wraps/skins • 2 medium sized dried Chinese mushrooms, soaked in hot water for 1 hour • 100g Chinese chives • 200g fillet of chicken • 2 tsp light soya sauce • ½ tsp sesame oil • 2 tsp cornflour • 2 tsp Chinese yellow wine or dry sherry • 3 tbsp vegetable oil • 1 tsp chopped ginger • 1 tsp chopped garlic • 400g bean sprouts, roots removed • 1 tsp salt • 1 egg white • 5 cups peanut oil

Method: Defrost spring roll wraps/skins for 20 minutes. Remove stems from mushrooms and slice caps thinly. Cut Chinese chives into thumb lengths. Slice fillet of chicken into fine julienne, marinate with light soya sauce, sesame oil, cornflour and wine and set aside. Heat 3 tablespoons vegetable oil and add ginger and garlic, stir frying well before adding beansprouts, mushrooms and chives and stir frying briefly. Stir in chicken and fry till cooked. Cool filling before adding to the wraps/skins, fold into spring rolls. Deep fry in hot oil till golden brown. Drain.

new ideas

Serving Spring Rolls as a dessert and baking them instead of deep frying are new twists to an age-old recipe. **SPRING HOME TYJ Spring Roll Pastry** can also be used without deep frying and the wrap can be rolled round so that one side is left open. Lining the spring roll wrap with lettuce before adding the filling makes for a beautiful presentation.

Each culture has its own top-of-the-line food items.
For the French and Europeans, it is Foie Gras,
Truffles and Caviar. In Asia, among the most
prized epicurean gourmet foods for the Chinese, is
the humble Bird's Nest, delicate in its gelatinous
texture and its even more elusive flavour.

Bird's Nest Deluxe

Preparation time: Nil   Cooking time: Nil   To serve: 1 - 4

1 bottle DRAGON BRAND Royal Concentrated Bird's Nest

For a truly luxurious gourmet experience, serve 1 bottle of **DRAGON BRAND Royal Concentrated Bird's Nest** for 1 person. For a spectacular effect at the dining table, serve 1 whole bottle, unopened, and present it on a silver platter, surrounded by uncooked bird's nest.

Food notes: This is a top quality product from DRAGON BRAND and is filled to the brim with genuine bird's nest. Once the bottle is opened, it must be stored in the fridge and the contents must be consumed within two weeks. **DRAGON BRAND Royal Concentrated Bird's Nest** can be consumed a teaspoon at a time each day. It comes in bottles of 150g nett.

Where available: DRAGON BRAND and other Kim Hing products can be found in Asia, Australia and the USA.

mother's hints for preparing and cooking bird's nest broth

Bird's nest is traditionally sold dried. It is the spittle of swifts, a bird species found along the coast of southern China and in South East Asia. The bird used its spittle to hold twigs together for its nests. Soak dried bird's nest in water overnight. Drain and carefully pick out any feathers and twigs with a pair of tweezers. Soak again and continue to remove the dirt till the bird's nest is totally clean. Drain and double boil in water and rock sugar to make a delicious, sweet dessert.

Cleaned and dried bird's nest

new ideas

Puree 100g each of rock melon and honeydew melon flesh separately. Flavour with orange or lemon sauce and arrange 1 layer of the green melon puree at the bottom of 4 dessert glasses. Put in the freezer for about 1 hour. Remove from the freezer and add the orange layer – freeze for 1 to 2 hours till the puree has become a firm slush. Top with the contents of half a bottle of **DRAGON BRAND Royal Concentrated Bird's Nest** and allow the dessert to sit for 15 to 20 minutes till the slush has melted a little. Garnish with melon balls.

Endless summer days beckon – it's great to spend time outdoors and enjoy a picnic in the sun. Salads, long cool drinks and Singapore chilli crabs make delicious fare and refreshments for activities in the great outdoors.

Summer...

Soy Sausage Delight

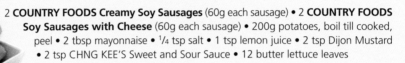

Preparation time: 20 minutes
Cooking time: 15 minutes

De-frosting time: 15 - 20 minutes
To serve: 4

2 **COUNTRY FOODS Creamy Soy Sausages** (60g each sausage) • 2 **COUNTRY FOODS Soy Sausages with Cheese** (60g each sausage) • 200g potatoes, boil till cooked, peel • 2 tbsp mayonnaise • ¼ tsp salt • 1 tsp lemon juice • 2 tsp Dijon Mustard • 2 tsp CHNG KEE'S Sweet and Sour Sauce • 12 butter lettuce leaves

De-frost the **COUNTRY FOODS Creamy Soy Sausages** and **COUNTRY FOODS Soy Sausages with Cheese** and then steam for 5 minutes. Set aside to cool. Alternatively, you can microwave the frozen sausages for 2 to 3 minutes. Slice sausages thinly on the diagonal. Dice the potatoes and add mayonnaise, salt and lemon juice. Divide the butter lettuce into 4 portions and place each portion on a plate. Top the lettuce with potato salad and arrange the sausages next to it. Dot the plates with Dijon mustard and sweet and sour sauce. Serve as a cold appetiser.

Food notes: Frozen **Soy Sausages by COUNTRY FOODS** are a delicious alternative to meat sausages and are ideal for vegetarians to enjoy. They come cooked and frozen in 1kg catering packs.

Where available: COUNTRY FOODS products can be found in Asia and the Middle East.

classic sweet and sour sauce

Preparation time: 15 minutes   Cooking time: 3 - 4 minutes   To serve: 4 - 6

Ingredients: ½ cup fresh or canned pineapple juice • 1 tbsp tomato ketchup, optional • 3 tbsp cornflour or corn starch • 1 cup water • ¼ cup sugar • ⅛ - ¼ tsp salt • ¼ cup rice or red wine vinegar • 3 tbsp lemon juice • 4 - 6 drops red food colouring or a few pinches of Chinese red food colouring powder

Method: Mix cornflour with ¼ cup of water and put aside. Put pineapple juice and tomato ketchup in a small saucepan. Add remaining water, sugar and salt and put on low heat. Stir constantly to dissolve the sugar and then add vinegar, lemon juice and cornflour mixture and stir well till it thickens. Add red food colouring to create the distinctive sweet and sour sauce colour. For Chinese red food colouring powder, dissolve it in the cornflour mixture before adding to the saucepan.

Butter lettuce, tomato and sweet and sour sauce

Soya beans are soaked in water till softened and ground into a fine paste to make a large variety of delicious dishes including vegetarian hamburgers and sausages.

new ideas

Soy Sausages by COUNTRY FOODS are great as a breakfast treat especially for vegetarians. It can be grilled and served with tomato ketchup or chilli sauce and accompanied by grilled tomatoes and crusty bread. They will also make an ideal dinner party treat cooked in a hearty farmer's stew with an Italian tomato ragu sauce.

Dried fruits and nuts served in its natural form offer a healthy choice as well as add a wide range of nutrients to your meal.

new ideas

Dried fruits and nuts are used for more than just fruit cakes and muffins. They are also widely used in appetiser salads. Not only are **TONG GARDEN All Natural Cocktail Snacks** a delectable vegetarian choice, it also makes a great salad when added to greens garnished with orange segments.

All Natural Salad Orientale

Preparation time: 15 minutes   Cooking time: Nil   To serve: 4

2 x 120g packets of **TONG GARDEN Delights All Natural Cocktail Snacks** (with figs, green raisins, black raisins, cashew nuts, almonds and pistachios) • 150g cherry tomatoes or normal sized tomatoes, cut into quarters • 1 stick celery (100g), sliced thinly on the diagonal • 1 onion (200g), finely julienned • 1 orange (250g), peeled and cut into segments • 2 butter lettuce or 2 cups of salad mix

Salad Dressing: $^1/_4$ cup rice vinegar • $1^1/_2$ tbsp light soya sauce • 1 tsp sesame oil • 4 tbsp plum sauce • 2 tbsp lemon sauce • 1 - 2 tsp Sichuan hot chilli sauce or paste (optional). Mix well.

Mix the **TONG GARDEN All Natural Cocktail Snacks** with salad dressing. Arrange vegetables and orange segments on a salad plate and top with the **TONG GARDEN All Natural Cocktail Snacks**-salad dressing mixture.

Food notes: TONG GARDEN All Natural Cocktail Snacks comes in a variety of combinations of dried fruit and nuts. They come in 120g packets and 128g and 148g canisters.

Where available: TONG GARDEN food products can be found in Africa, the Asia Pacific and the Middle East.

traditional nut and fruit muffin

Preparation time: 20 minutes   Cooking time: 25 minutes
To make: 10 - 20 muffins

Ingredients: 1 packet (120g) mixed nuts and dried fruits • 120g black raisins • $^3/_4$ cup sunflower oil • $^1/_2$ cup fine sugar • 1 tsp vanilla essence • 2 eggs, lightly beaten • 3 ripe bananas (300g unpeeled weight), peeled and mashed • 2 cups (250g) plain flour • $^3/_4$ tsp baking soda • 1 tbsp baking powder • $^1/_4$ tsp salt

Method: Pre-heat oven to 175 degrees Celsius. Roughly chop the nuts and raisins. Put aside. In a bowl, mix oil, sugar, vanilla essence, eggs and bananas. Sift flour, baking soda, baking powder and salt into the banana mixture and mix well. Fold in chopped nuts, fruit and raisins. Pour batter into paper muffin cups, only filling $^3/_4$ of each cup. Bake for 25 to 30 minutes in a pre-heated oven at 180 degrees Celsius. When it is done, a skewer driven through the centre of the muffin will come out clean.

*Fish quenelles, known as fish balls, are
a popular source of protein in Singapore.
Along with squid quenelles, they are
precooked and are featured in a
fascinating array of seafood offerings.*

new ideas Serving **DODO Seafood Treats** with a Mayonnaise Wasabi Sauce is a new take on an all time favourite. The seafood balls can also be sliced into fine juliennes and fried with rice or noodles.

Oriental Fish Quenelle Sampler

Preparation time: 30 minutes   Cooking time: 3 - 4 minutes   To serve: 4

4 **DODO Seafood Treats Otah Fish Cake** • 4 **DODO Seafood Treats Crab Flavoured Balls** • 4 **DODO Seafood Treats Crab Flavoured Cake** • 2 handfuls of mixed salad greens • 8 asparagus sticks, lightly blanched in boiling water • 4 spring onion (scallion) stalks, lightly blanched in boiling water • 1 Nori (seaweed) sheet • 1 clove garlic, peeled, sliced and deep fried • 1 cucumber, cut into short strips • 1 hard boiled quail's egg • 2 stalks edible flowers, optional • 4 tbsp mayonnaise • 1$\frac{1}{2}$ tsp prepared wasabi paste

Steam the frozen **DODO Seafood Treats** selection of products for 3 to 4 minutes till heated through. Set aside to cool to room temperature. Serve 1 of each type per person. Decorate each serving platter with half a handful of salad greens. Use only the tips of the asparagus. Tie 2 asparagus tips together with a spring onion stalk and trim the stalk. Cut the sides of the DODO Seafood Treats Otah Fish Cake to form a clean square shape and decorate with the asparagus bundle. Cut the Nori sheet into strips and use a strip of Nori to tie around each DODO Seafood Treats Crab Flavoured Ball, and top with 1 slice of fried garlic and a cucumber garnish. Top the DODO Seafood Treats Crab Flavoured Cake with a quarter of a quail's egg and an edible flower. Mix mayonnaise with wasabi and serve with the DODO Seafood Treats.

Food notes: DODO Seafood Treats products are frozen and should be steamed while still frozen for fresh flavour.

Where available: DODO and other Thong Siek food products can be found in the Asia Pacific, Europe and the USA.

home-made fish balls (oriental fish quenelles)

Preparation time: 1 hour   Resting time: 1 - 3 hours
Cooking time: 3 - 4 minutes

Ingredients: 1kg whole Wolf Herring (Chirocentrus Dorab and known as Ikan Parang in the Malay language) or whole Yellowtail or 500g fillet of fish • 1$\frac{1}{2}$ tsp salt • 180 - 200ml iced water • $\frac{1}{2}$ tsp finely ground white pepper • 2 to 3 tsp tapioca flour or cornflour (cornstarch) • 3 litres (12 cups) ice water mixed with 2 tsp of fine salt

Method: Debone the fish and scrape the meat from the skin of the fish fillet with a spoon. Add salt, half of the water, pepper and flour to fish, mix well, stir in the remaining water in small measures. When mixture is firm, put into a large bowl, scoop up the mixture and throw it against the inside of the bowl. Repeat 50 to 60 times. Squeeze the fish meat through the thumb and forefinger to form a ball and scoop with a spoon into a bowl of salted iced water. Refrigerate for 2 hours. Boil till cooked.

Yellowtail

*The Singapore Chilli Crab is an
East Coast seafood tradition.
Over 50 years ago, this famed dish
was created under the swaying seafront
coconut leaves, drawing crowds to
this beach-side location.*

new
ideas   This chilli crab recipe can be used with mussels, lobsters or prawns. You can also put all the seafood together for a seafood stew. **HAI'S Chilli Crab Sauce** also makes a good accompaniment to fried battered fish as well as Fish and Chips.

Chilli Crabs Singapura

Preparation time: 25 minutes   Cooking time: 15 - 18 minutes   To serve: 2

2 tbsp vegetable oil • 1 packet **HAI'S Chilli Crab Sauce** • 1 whole crab, prepared for cooking, or 6 crab claws • 300ml water • 1 egg, beaten • 2 spring onions (30g), cut into finger lengths, optional

Heat oil in the wok, add one packet of **HAI's Chilli Crab Sauce** and fry until fragrant. Put the crabs in and stir fry till crabs turn red, add 300ml of water and cover the wok. Simmer on medium heat for about 15 minutes. Stir in beaten egg and spring onions. Serve with slices of baguette and a side salad. If the claws have not been cracked, give each diner a nut cracker.

Food notes: HAI's Chilli Crab Sauce comes in packets of 200g.

Where available: HAI's products can be found in Asia.

traditional east coast chilli crab

Preparation time: 50 minutes   Cooking time: 20 minutes   To serve: 2

Ingredients for crab: 8 cloves garlic • 8 fresh red chillies • 3 tbsp vegetable oil • 1 large crab, prepared for cooking • 1 egg • 2 spring onion (scallions) plants, cut into finger lengths • 1 tsp freshly squeezed lime or lemon juice • 1 small bunch coriander (cilantro) plant, cut into 2cm long pieces

Method: Pound or process garlic and chillies to a rough paste. Heat oil in a wok or shallow saucepan over high heat. Add garlic and chilli paste and fry for 3 to 4 minutes till fragrant. Add crabs and stir fry for 3 to 4 minutes until the shells turn slightly red. Add sauce. Stir well, cover the wok and simmer for 10 minutes till the shells turn bright red which indicates that the crabs are cooked. Break egg into the sauce and mix well. Simmer for another 10 seconds. Turn off the heat and stir in spring onions and lime or lemon juice. Garnish with coriander leaves and serve.

For traditional Chilli Crab sauce, whisk all the following ingredients together and set aside: 1 cup water • 5 tbsp tomato ketchup • 1 1/2 - 3 tbsp sugar, or according to taste • 1 1/2 tsp cornflour • 1 tsp pounded brown preserved soya beans or dark miso, optional • 1/4 tsp salt

To prepare crabs: Mud crabs, readily available in Singapore, are bought while still alive. Kill the crab by piercing the underside with a knife. Peel off the shell and chop the body into 4 to 8 pieces. Twist off the claws and crack them. Wash well and drain.

Fresh red chillies and small bird's eye chillies

noodle sauce traditional

Preparation time: 20 minutes + 2 hours soaking time   Cooking time: 10 minutes
To serve: 2 - 3

Ingredients: 2 dried mushrooms • 1 tbsp oyster sauce • 1 tbsp light soya sauce • 1 tsp dark soya sauce • ½ tsp sesame oil • 1 tsp sugar • 1 tsp cornflour, mixed with 3 tbsp water • 2 - 3 tbsp oil • 3 cloves garlic, finely chopped • 60g Chinese yellow chives, cut into 3cm lengths • pre-prepared noodles

Method: Wash dried mushrooms and soak in warm water for 1 to 2 hours till softened. Squeeze out the water, cut and discard the hard stalk, slice the cap into fine strips and keep aside. Mix oyster sauce, light and dark soya sauce, sesame oil, and sugar and cornflour mixture. Set aside. Heat oil and fry mushrooms for 2 to 3 minutes, add garlic and fry till garlic is slightly brown. Add sauce mixture and stir till the sauce simmers and thickens a little. Stir in the chives and pour over prepared noodles.

Instant noodles

new ideas

For something really different, cooked **KOKA Instant Stir-Fry Original Flavour Noodles** can be wrapped in a large omelette and presented at the table as a novel dish. Make a criss-cross slit on top of the omelette, peel the omelette sides back to reveal the noodles below. Serve with the crab sticks on the side.

Tasty Noodles Deluxe

Preparation time: 5 minutes   Cooking time: 3 minutes   To serve: 1

1 packet **KOKA Instant Stir-Fry Original Flavour Noodles** • 350ml water • 2 DODO Seafood Treats frozen Crab Sticks • 1 DODO Seafood Treats frozen Mini Chikuwa • 50g spinach, optional

Boil **KOKA Instant Stir-Fry Original Flavour Noodles** in water for 3 minutes and drain the noodles. Keep half of the water aside. Empty ¾ of the contents of the seasoning sachet over the noodles and toss well quickly. If the noodles seem too dry, add 1 to 2 tablespoons of water. Empty the remaining quarter of the seasoning into the boiling water and stir well. Steam or microwave the frozen crab sticks and mini chikuwa till warmed through. Serve the noodles in a large noodle bowl with finely shredded mini crab sticks and mini chikuwa skewered on a chopstick. Pour the gravy into the bowl. If desired, blanch spinach and add to the noodles. This deluxe version looks and tastes good and is a crowd pleaser.

Food notes: Each packet of **KOKA Instant Noodles** serves 1 person. There is a wide range of Koka noodle flavours.

Where available: KOKA products by Tat Hui Foods can be found in the Asia Pacific, Canada, Europe, the Middle East and the USA.

Instant noodles are a must-have in the Singapore pantry and are a staple of late-night supper meals - that time when hunger strikes and you need an instant treat to pep you up. Just three minutes and a hot, piping delicious meal is ready.

One of Singapore's most iconic and loved street foods is the seemingly simple Chicken Rice. One whiff of the delicious aroma of the steaming rice is enough to arouse the most intense culinary excitement!

new ideas

CHNG KEE'S Hainanese Chicken Rice Mix can be used to create delicious dishes in a very short time. Stir fry 500g of vegetables with 1 to 2 tablespoons of CHNG KEE'S Chicken Rice Mix for a delicious dish. Another simple method is to steam 500g of cubed or sliced chicken breast and legs with 2 to 3 tablespoons of the mix. There is no need to add any other seasoning.

Singapore Chicken Rice

Preparation time: 15 minutes   Cooking time: 1 hour, including boiling time
To serve: 6 - 8

4 cups (600g) uncooked long grain rice, washed and drained • 750ml water • $^1/_2$ bottle **CHNG KEE'S Hainanese Chicken Rice Mix** • 1 whole chicken about 1.2kg or 2 chicken breasts • 4 tbsp CHNG KEE'S Garlic Ginger Chilli Sauce • 4 tbsp CHNG KEE'S Freshly Minced Ginger mixed with 1 tbsp of chopped spring onions • 4 tbsp CHNG KEE'S Dark Soya Sauce • $^1/_2$ cucumber • 2 cherry tomatoes

Add **CHNG KEE'S Hainanese Chicken Rice Mix** to rice and water in a rice cooker. When the rice is cooked, stir gently with a fork and cover the rice cooker for 10 minutes before serving. In the meantime, boil a large pot of water and add chicken, breast side down. Cover and poach on low heat for about 30 minutes, making sure that the water does not come to the full boil. The chicken will be cooked al dente. Remove from the water and put chicken into an ice water bath. When the chicken is cold, remove from the water, pat dry and de-bone. Cut into thin slices and serve with rice. You can also put the rice in banana leaf cones. Serve with the 3 sauces and garnish with cucumber and tomato.

Food notes: Each bottle of **CHNG KEE'S Hainanese Chicken Rice Mix** contains 240ml (220g) of mix.

Where available: CHNG KEE'S and other Sin Hwa Dee products can be found in Asia, Europe and the Middle East.

traditional mother's chicken rice

Preparation time: 1$^1/_2$ hours   Cooking time: 1$^1/_2$ hours   To serve: 6 - 8

Ingredients: 1 chicken (about 1.2 kg) • 1 plant spring onion, washed and cleaned • 4 slices fresh ginger, peeled • 3 litres water mixed with 2 tsp salt • 6 tbsp vegetable oil • 6 - 8 cloves garlic, finely chopped • 20g Lengkuas (Galangal, also known as blue ginger) • 4 pandan leaves • 4 cups long-grain uncooked rice, washed and drained • 1 tsp fine salt

Method: Stuff the cavity of the chicken with the spring onion plant and ginger. Boil the salted water in a large pot. Add chicken to the boiling water, breast side down. Simmer at just under boiling point and cook, covered, for about 30 to 40 minutes. Drain chicken and put in ice water bath. Drain and cut into serving pieces.

To Prepare Rice: Heat the oil in a wok or saucepan over high heat. Add the garlic and Galangal and stir fry till fragrant. Add pandan leaves and the uncooked rice grains and stir fry for 1 to 2 minutes till fragrant. Transfer to a rice cooker and add salt and 3 to 3$^1/_4$ cups of the hot chicken soup and steam till cooked.

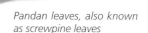

Pandan leaves, also known as screwpine leaves

A hot favourite in fine Chinese restaurants is the Mango Pudding, a delicate oriental-style jelly usually served with evaporated milk.

new ideas

UNICURD I'sojoy Soy Dessert can be served with fresh fruits, a squeeze of lime juice and herbs like kaffir lime leaves or mint leaves to create a refreshing dessert after a heavy meal.

47

Mango Beancurd

Preparation time: 5 minutes   Cooking time: Nil   To serve: 4

4 packs of chilled **UNICURD I'sojoy Soy Dessert with Natural Mango Extracts** •
1 mango • 1 kaffir lime leaf, optional

Peel off the plastic cover of the packets of **UNICURD I'sojoy Soy Dessert**. Gently turn
the pack upside down and squeeze the sides of the plastic container so that the jelly-like
soy dessert will slip out of the packet. Serve well chilled with diced mangos and finely
chopped kaffir lime leaves. You can also serve this dessert with some honey for a sweeter
flavour.

Food notes: UNICURD I'sojoy Soy Dessert comes in packs of 180g and is to be stored
at between 2 to 7 degrees Celsius.

Where available: I'sojoy and other UNICURD food products can be found in Asia, Europe
and the USA.

traditional mango pudding

Preparation time: 45 minutes   Cooking time: 15 minutes Chilling
time: 3 - 4 hours   To serve: 4 - 6

Ingredients: 1 packet agar agar powder (12g) • 300g fine sugar
• ½ litre water • 2 cans evaporated milk or 3½ cups soya bean milk
• A little yellow colouring, optional • 3 ripe mangoes • 5 egg whites
• 1 can evaporated milk for serving

Method: Mix agar agar powder with sugar and water, stir well and boil.
Let the mixture cool, add 2 cans evaporated milk OR 3½ cups soya bean milk
and food colouring. Dice flesh of 1 mango and puree the other 2 mangoes. Beat
egg whites till stiff. Mix mango puree into agar agar and fold in egg whites. Pour into
jelly moulds, chill till set, unmould and serve with diced mango and extra evaporated milk.

Mango

traditional soya bean milk

Preparation time: 1 hour   Cooking time: 30 minutes   Soaking time: 8 hours

Ingredients: 250g dried soya beans soaked overnight in water • 9 cups water

Method: Soaked soya beans will weigh 650g and makes about 3 to 3¼ cups. Mix each cup
with 3 cups of water. Liquefy the soaked soya bean and water mixture and bring to boil in
a large pot. A lot of froth will form as the mixture boils. Constant stirring is needed to prevent
the froth from boiling over. Boil mixture for 20 minutes till there is no froth. Strain the mixture
over a cheese cloth and discard the pulp. Serve hot or chilled. Add sugar to taste.

One of the most beloved of dried flower teas is the
chrysanthemum, treasured for its cooling properties
to counter the intense heat of the summer sun.

Summer Chrysanthemum Ice

Preparation time: 5 minutes   Freezing time: 4 - 6 hours   To serve: 4

5 sachets **OWL Instant Chrysanthemum Tea with Honey** • 300ml water • 200g canned or fresh lychees, peeled and de-seeded or honeydew and rock melon cubes or pear and apple cubes

Mix **OWL Instant Chrysanthemum Tea with Honey** and 300ml of hot water till the tea granules are dissolved. Let mixture cool, put in a shallow pan and place in the freezer for 4 hours to 8 hours. The sugar in the tea will prevent the liquid from being frozen solid and instead turn it into a rough grained shaved ice. Put the fruits into 4 dessert bowls; remove the iced chrysanthemum tea by scraping it with a spoon. Top the fruits with the chrysanthemum ice shavings. Serve at once as a refreshing dessert.

Food notes: Each sachet of **OWL Instant Chrysanthemum Tea with Honey** weighs 18g and makes a refreshing beverage when mixed with 1 cup of water. It can be drunk hot or cold. Chrysanthemum tea is one of the more popular beverages to accompany a Chinese meal.

Where available: OWL International products can be found in Asia, Europe, the Middle East and the USA.

traditional chrysanthemum tea with honey

Preparation time: 10 minutes   Cooking time: Nil
To serve: 4 - 6

Ingredients: ¹/₂ cup dried chrysanthemum tea (dried chrysanthemum flowers) • 4 cups boiling water • 4 tbsp honey

Method: Rinse a teapot with boiling water and drain. Add chrysanthemum tea and pour in boiling water. Cover teapot and allow the tea to infuse for 3 to 4 minutes. Add honey to taste. Serve. You can make a second brew by pouring more boiling water into the teapot of chrysanthemum. The second brew will be slightly weaker than the first.

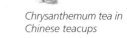

Chrysanthemum tea in Chinese teacups

new ideas

OWL Instant Chrysanthemum Tea with Honey can be mixed with gelatine or agar agar powder and made into a delicate jelly dessert. Add diced canned lychees or longans and allow to solidify in a fancy jelly mould to create a spectacular dessert display.

traditional singapore rojak

Preparation time: 30 minutes   Cooking time: Nil   To serve: 4

Ingredients: 2 tbsp tamarind pulp (Assam) • 4 tbsp water • 1 lime, squeezed for juice • 2 tbsp Hay Ko (thick black prawn paste) • 2 - 3 tbsp sugar • 1/2 tbsp chilli paste • 4 tbsp roughly ground toasted peanuts • 100g sweet turnips, peeled and cut into wedges • 100g cucumbers, cut into wedges, and discard the soft core • 100g pineapple flesh, cut into wedges • 1 fried dough fritter, optional, cut into 2cm lengths • 2 tau pok (deep fried bean curd puffs), cut into quarters

Method: Mix tamarind pulp with water and squeeze out the juice, discard the pulp. Mix in lime juice and Hay Ko; stir well to dissolve the thick Hay Ko. Add sugar and chilli paste to taste. Toss in the peanuts, vegetables, pineapple, dough fritters and tau pok and mix thoroughly. It is traditionally served on a banana leaf.

new ideas

Dessert fruit salad served with **KWONG CHEONG THYE Rojak (Vegetarian) Sauce** is a novel idea.

Fruit Fantasia with a Rojak and Orange Strawberry Sauce

Preparation time: 20 minutes   Cooking time: Nil   To serve: 4

80g rock melon flesh • 50g star fruit • 1 nectarine or peach • 6 strawberries • 1/4 cup **KWONG CHEONG THYE Orange Sauce** • 1/2 tbsp cornflour mixed with 2 tbsp water • 1 sachet (150g) **KWONG CHEONG THYE Rojak (Vegetarian) Sauce** mixed with juice from 1 lime

Use a melon baller to make melon balls. Slice star fruit and cut nectarine into wedges. Puree strawberries with orange sauce and mix with cornflour mixture. Heat the sauce over a medium fire till it thickens. Remove from heat, cool in the fridge. Arrange the fruits on a platter and serve with the two sauces – the fruit sauce and the Rojak sauce.

Food notes: 1 packet of **KWONG CHEONG THYE Singapore Rojak (Vegetarian) Sauce** contains 2 sachets of 150g each of sauce and serves 2 persons.

Where available: KWONG CHEONG THYE products can be found in Asia, Europe, the Middle East and the USA.

Rojak is a favourite salad with a delectable sauce made with thick prawn paste, chillies, peanuts, sugar and tamarind juice. It is traditionally eaten during lunch or dinner or as a snack.

It's time to enjoy the brilliant colours
of autumn and the rich harvest of the soil.
Dining takes on a heavier and richer tone to
counter the nip in the cold night air.

Autumn...

Singapore's Satay Club moved from its home in Beach Road to the Esplanade and then to Clarke Quay. But you do not need a club to enjoy satay - just wait for a great moonlit night, fire up the barbecue and enjoy a satay feast outdoors, under the stars.

new ideas

PRIMA TASTE Singapore Satay Sauce can be used as a dip for vegetable salads. The classic Singapore Malay salad is Gado Gado which contains julienne of cabbage, blanched long beans, deep fried bean curd, deep fried 'tempeh' (fermented whole soya bean cakes), boiled potatoes and eggs. Add a new twist to this traditional dish by serving the sauce in a butter lettuce leaf cup and grating hard boiled egg over the top of the sauce. You can also create your own unique salad to complement the satay sauce.

Singapore Satay

Preparation time: 30 minutes   Marinating time: 6 hours   To serve: 4
Cooking time: 10 minutes

350g chicken breast meat (makes 16 sticks of Satay) • 1 box **PRIMA TASTE Ready-To-Cook Meal Kit for Singapore Satay** • 4 tbsp vegetable oil • 16 satay sticks or bamboo skewers • 150 - 200ml water • 1 cucumber • 1 carrot • 1 onion, optional

Cut chicken into small cubes and add Singapore Satay marinade from the PRIMA TASTE Ready-To-Cook Meal Kit. Keep in the fridge for 6 hours. Skewer 3 pieces of chicken onto each stick. To prepare the sauce, pour the contents of the sachet of Singapore Satay sauce mix into a small saucepan with 150ml water and heat till nearly boiling before adding 2 tablespoons vegetable oil. Stir well. Mix in the Singapore Satay peanut paste and bring to boil over medium heat. When a layer of oil forms on top, it is cooked. Add water if the sauce is too thick. Put aside. Brush skewers of chicken satay with remaining oil and barbecue over charcoal for 2 to 3 minutes on each side or grill on a pan till cooked. Serve with sauce, cucumber, carrot sticks and wedges of onion.

Food notes: PRIMA TASTE Ready-To-Cook Meal Kit for Singapore Satay comes in 275g boxes and contains 1 foil sachet each of Singapore Satay marinade, Singapore Satay sauce and Singapore Satay peanut paste.

Where available: PRIMA FOODS products can be found in Asia, Australia, Canada, the USA and the UK.

traditional east coast satay sauce

Preparation time: 40 minutes   Cooking time: 25 minutes
To serve: 6

Ingredients: 60g tamarind pulp (Assam) • 2 cups water • $1/2$ cup vegetable oil • 1 cup finely ground roasted peanuts • $1/4$ cup sugar • $1/2$ tbsp rice vinegar or malt vinegar • $3/4$ tsp salt • 1 stalk lemon grass, crushed lightly

Spice Mixture: 3 candlenuts • 15g Lengkuas (Galangal and also known as blue ginger) • 15 dried chillies, soaked in hot water for 1 hour till softened • 3 cloves garlic, peeled • 1 tsp shrimp paste (belachan), optional • 30g peeled shallots

Method: Mix tamarind pulp with water and strain, discard pulp. Pound or grind spice mixture till very fine. Fry spice mixture in hot oil till fragrant. Add tamarind liquid and remaining ingredients. Boil for 15 minutes, stir well. Cool for 30 minutes before serving.

clockwise from left:
Lengkuas, candlenuts
and turmeric

Lemon grass

Dim Sum Medley

Preparation time: 10 minutes   Cooking time: 10 minutes   To serve: 4

8 Xing Food Exotic Asian Food Cabbage Roll • 4 **Xing Food Exotic Asian Food Seaweed Corn Rolls** • 8 **Xing Food Exotic Asian Food Chicken Swee Kao** • 1 - 1$\frac{1}{2}$ cups chicken broth • 1 tsp light soya sauce • $\frac{1}{8}$ tsp sesame oil

The pre-cooked frozen dim sum must be kept at -18 degrees Celsius. Steam while still frozen for freshness. Steam the **Xing Food Exotic Asian Food Cabbage Roll** and the Seaweed Corn Rolls for about 5 to 6 minutes on high heat till the dim sum are heated right through. Boil a pot of water and add the frozen Chicken Swee Kao and boil till the Swee Kao float. Alternatively, they can be steamed till heated right through. In the meantime, heat chicken broth with soya sauce and sesame oil and place in 4 deep platters. Put 2 cabbage rolls, 1 seaweed corn roll and 2 Chicken Swee Kao in each platter of broth. Alternatively, you could serve each type of dim sum individually in small bowls.

Food notes: Xing Food Exotic Asian Food by Sin Mui Heng Food Industries is sold to the catering industry and is usually packed frozen in boxes and shipped frozen as well. Many of the **Xing Food Exotic Asian Food** dim sum items are wrapped in bean curd skin and are usually deep fried. We experimented with steaming them for a healthier choice and discovered that they taste as delicious steamed as they do when fried.

Where available: Xing Food Exotic Asian Food and other Sin Mui Heng products can be found in Australia, Brunei, Canada and the Maldives.

traditional mother's cabbage rolls

Preparation time: 40 minutes   Cooking time: 20 minutes   To serve: 8 rolls

Ingredients: 8 Tientsin (Chinese) cabbage leaves, blanched lightly • 8 spring onion stalks, blanched lightly • 150g chicken meat, finely chopped • 100g prawn meat, finely diced • 3 water chestnuts, peeled and chopped • 2 tbsp finely chopped spring onions • $\frac{1}{4}$ tsp fine salt • 1 tsp light soya sauce • 2 tsp oyster sauce • 1 tsp sesame oil

Method: Pat the Tientsin cabbage leaves with paper towels till dry. Cut off about 2 cm of the hard stalk and trim the top of the leaf in a straight line. Mix all the other ingredients, except spring onion stalks, together to form the filling. Put about 2 tablespoons of filling across the centre of each Tientsin cabbage leaf, fold over and cover the filling completely, spring roll style. Trim off the excess leaf if the roll is too bulky. Tie each roll with 1 spring onion stalk and steam the cabbage rolls for 6 to 8 minutes over medium heat till cooked. Serve.

Water chestnuts

Dim Sum are small appetisers very much like tapas and they belong to traditional Canton cuisine in China. They are usually served in small bamboo steamer baskets or platters.

new ideas

Our Dim Sum Medley recipe where **Xing Food Exotic Asian Food** dim sum are served in individual portions and in a bed of delicate broth presents a new idea for serving this all time favourite – they are traditionally served without broth in portions of three of each item.

Rice is the main staple in Asia. Noodles and vermicelli made with rice are popular in Singapore, and are featured in dishes of our three main ethnic groups: Chinese, Malay and Indian.

traditional vegetarian singapore noodles

Preparation time: 30 minutes   Soaking time: 2 hours   Cooking time: 20 minutes   To serve: 5

Ingredients: 1 packet (300g) rice vermicelli or brown rice vermicelli • 10 cloves garlic, peeled, finely chopped • ½ cup vegetable oil • 6 stalks leeks, finely sliced • 3 large onions, finely sliced • 400g carrots, peeled, finely shredded • 400g cabbage, finely shredded • 20 fresh Shitake or button mushrooms, finely sliced • 3 - 5 tbsp light soya sauce • 3 tbsp vegetarian oyster sauce, optional

Method: Soak rice vermicelli or brown rice vermicelli in water till soft. Drain. Heat oil in wok and fry garlic till fragrant. Add leeks, onions, carrots, and cabbage and mushrooms one at a time cooking each for a minute. Add 2 tablespoons light soya sauce and 1 tablespoon vegetarian oyster sauce, mix well and remove ¼ of the vegetables for garnishing. Add remaining light soya sauce, vegetarian oyster sauce and rice vermicelli to the wok. Stir fry for 10 minutes on medium heat till vermicelli is cooked. Garnish and serve.

Tientsin Cabbage Rolls with Brown Rice Vermicelli

Preparation time: 20 minutes   Cooking time: 5 - 10 minutes   To serve: 4

Ingredients: 100g **PEACOCK BRAND Brown Rice Vermicelli** • 12 whole Tientsin cabbage leaves, lightly blanched and patted dry • 150g bean sprouts, roots removed • 150g Enoki mushrooms, lightly blanched and patted dry • 1 carrot, peeled and julienned • 1 cucumber, peeled and cut into finger length juliennes • 1 handful coriander leaves

Method: Soak the dried **PEACOCK BRAND Brown Rice Vermicelli** in tap water for 1 minute, blanch in boiling water till soft, and wash in cold water and drain. Spread 1 Tientsin cabbage leaf on a dry cloth. Put half a handful of raw bean sprouts in a row of about 5 to 6 cm. Top with a handful of **PEACOCK BRAND Brown Rice Vermicelli**, add about a quarter of a handful each of the mushrooms, carrots, cucumber and 1 or 2 coriander leaves. Roll the cabbage leaf tightly, spring roll style. Cut each cabbage roll into 2 on the diagonal and arrange on a platter. Serve with Hoi Sin Tamarind Sauce.

Food notes: **PEACOCK BRAND Brown Rice Vermicelli** comes in packets of 300g each.

Where available: PEACOCK BRAND and other Chye Choon products can be found in Asia, Australia, Canada and the USA.

Delicious additions: We have created a novel vegetarian dish which can be enhanced with steamed taro or steamed sweet potatoes, peeled and cut into finger length sticks. Steamed chicken juliennes and peeled steamed prawns can also be added to the filling.

Hoi Sin Tamarind Sauce: 120ml hoi sin sauce • 50g tamarind paste mixed with 1/2 cup water and squeezed for juice, discard pulp and seeds • 100g crunchy peanut butter • 50g fine sugar • 3 cloves garlic, finely chopped

Method: Mix all the ingredients together to form a dipping sauce.

new ideas Create a delicious dessert with **PEACOCK BRAND Brown Rice Vermicelli**. Soak 100g rice vermicelli and boil till cooked. Drain well and leave to dry. Lightly toss with 2 tablespoons cornflour or tapioca flour and divide into 10 portions. Loosely pack each portion into a small coffee cup. Steam for 2 to 3 minutes till the flour is cooked. Leave the vermicelli 'dumplings' to cool and serve with coconut cream and Gula Melaka (palm sugar) sauce or cream and caramel sauce.

Roast Pumpkin with Mock Duck and Black Pepper Sauce

Preparation time: 30 minutes   Cooking time: 40 minutes (including roasting time)
To serve: 4

1 bottle **KWONG CHEONG THYE Black Pepper Crab Sauce** • ¹/₄ cup water • 1 can (280g) CIXIN Vegetarian Mock Braised Duck • 600g pumpkin • 200g pea shoots or Dou Miao, blanched in boiling water for a few seconds and drained • ¹/₂ tomato, seeds removed, finely diced • garnish of dried herbs and freshly crushed peppercorns

Dilute **KWONG CHEONG THYE Black Pepper Crab Sauce** with ¹/₄ cup water. Drain the canned mock duck. Heat mock duck with ³/₄ of the black pepper crab sauce in the microwave for 2 to 3 minutes or by light poaching for about 10 minutes. Remove from sauce and slice into ¹/₂ cm slices. In the meantime, cut pumpkin into 8 segments, discard seeds and soft pulp and roast in a pre-heated oven at 180 degrees Celsius for 25 to 30 minutes till cooked. Arrange 3 slices of mock duck, 2 slices of pumpkin, green vegetables and tomato cubes on each plate. Spoon the sauce over the pumpkin and mock duck and garnish with a sprinkling of cracked black peppercorns and the dried herbs.

Food notes: KWONG CHEONG THYE Black Pepper Crab Sauce comes in 230g bottles and 300g packets. Mock duck is made from wheat gluten and is part of the Chinese vegetarian culinary tradition.

Where available: KWONG CHEONG THYE products can be found in Asia, Europe, the Middle East and the USA.

traditional black pepper sauce

Preparation time: 20 minutes   Cooking time: 7 minutes   To serve: 4

Ingredients: 3 - 4 tbsp fresh roughly ground black peppercorns • 3 - 4 tbsp butter or vegetable oil • 10 cloves garlic, peeled and chopped • 10 slices young ginger • 1 - 2 tbsp oyster sauce • 2 tsp dark soya sauce • 1 tsp cornflour mixed with 3 tbsp water

Method: Dry-fry ground black peppercorns in a wok or frying pan for 2 to 3 minutes till fragrant. Remove and keep aside. Heat wok or frying pan, add butter and as it melts, add garlic and ginger and stir fry for 3 minutes till the mixture is fragrant. Add oyster sauce, soya sauce and cornflour mixture and bring to boil. Add peppercorns and stir till the sauce thickens.

Oyster sauce and white and black peppercorns

Vegetarians will find their culinary repertoire expand dramatically with Tasty Singapore's sauces, gluten creations, pastes and dips. An exciting taste journey awaits!

new ideas

Serving **KWONG CHEONG THYE Black Pepper Crab Sauce** over roasted pumpkin and mock duck creates an innovative new dish. The sauce also makes an ideal dip for Beef Fondue. Black pepper crab sauce is usually used for the classic Singapore dish of Black Pepper Crabs.

Fried rice takes on a delicious twist in Singapore's Nasi Goreng, the Malay-inspired version of the all-time favourite. A spicy chilli paste adds a delectable new flavour.

Nasi Goreng Singapore

Preparation time: 15 minutes   Cooking time: 30 minutes   To serve: 2

1 packet **YAMIE Yam Rice** • 330ml water • 1 cucumber • 3 tbsp vegetable oil • 2 eggs, beaten • 150g chicken breast meat, cut into cubes • 200g shrimps, peeled • 2 - 3 tbsp KWONG CHEONG THYE Premium Chilli King Sauce • ¼ tsp fine salt

Put uncooked **YAMIE Yam Rice** in a rice cooker. Fill the packet with water to reach the 330ml mark on the packet. Add to rice and cook for 15 minutes till cooked. Leave at 'warm' setting for 5 more minutes. Turn off heat, stir rice gently and thoroughly. Leave skin on cucumber, discard soft pulp and seeds and cut into small cubes. Heat wok, add 2 tablespoons oil, and add the eggs and scramble for 1 minute till lightly cooked. Remove eggs. Heat remaining oil, stir fry chicken over high heat for 30 seconds, and add shrimps and fry till cooked. Add cooked rice, KWONG CHEONG THYE Premium Chilli King Sauce and salt, and fry for 7 to 8 minutes till the rice is fragrant and dry. Add cucumber, stir well and serve.

Food notes: 1 packet of **YAMIE Yam Rice** weighs 220g and serves 2 persons. Ingredients include rice dried shrimps, mushrooms, yam, sesame oil, garlic and onions.

Where available: YAMIE and other Gan Hup Lee products can be found in the USA.

traditional sambal hay bee

Preparation time: 30 minutes   Cooking time: 10 minutes
To serve: 2 - 3

Ingredients: 80g dried prawns • 5 fresh red chillies • 2 tsp Belachan (shrimp paste) • 3 cloves garlic, peeled • 5 shallots, peeled • 6 tbsp vegetable oil

Method: Wash dried prawns and soak in warm water for 15 minutes till softened. Pound or blend in food processor till very fine. Keep aside. Process or pound the red chillies, Belachan, garlic and shallots till fine. Heat 5 tablespoons of oil over high heat. Stir fry dried prawns for 4 to 5 minutes till cooked and until it exudes oil. Push the dried prawns to one side of the wok. Add 1 tablespoon of oil and when it is hot, add the spice paste, stir fry for 5 minutes over medium heat till the spices are well cooked and exudes oil. Stir in the prawns and fry. The Sambal Hay Bee can be used to replace the Premium Chilli King Sauce.

Shrimp paste also known as Belachan

new ideas

YAMIE Yam Rice is full of flavour and makes a delicious accompaniment to roast duck, grilled fillet steak or Japanese Beef Yakiniku. Just add a serving of vegetables to complete the meal.

Beef Rendang is a popular dish especially during Malay festivals. It is often featured as the star dish at celebrations like Eid, which heralds the end of the Muslim fasting month.

new ideas

Rendang lends the Singapore flavour to French pastry when thick **AMOCAN Premium Singapore Rendang Sauce** is mixed with sliced mushrooms and added to the filling of an elegant beef roll.

Beef Rendang

Preparation time: 10 minutes   Cooking time: 1 - 3 hours   To serve: 4

300g sirloin or shin of beef, cut into chunks or thick slices • 1 can **AMOCAN Premium Singapore Rendang Sauce** • 2 tbsp vegetable oil • 1 - 2 cups water • 3 kaffir lime leaves, optional • $^1/_4$ tsp salt, optional

Marinate 300g beef with half of the **AMOCAN Premium Singapore Rendang Sauce** and refrigerate for $^1/_2$ hour. Stir-fry meat in 2 tablespoons oil, add remaining sauce, 1 cup of water and kaffir lime leaves and bring to boil. Turn heat down to medium low and simmer till the meat is tender. Sirloin will take about 1 hour while shin beef will take 2 to 3 hours. For the shin beef, add 1 more cup of water. Serve with SUNBEAM Garlic Rice pressed into a cone shape to resemble the traditional Malay Nasi Tumpang festive rice dish.

Food notes: Each can of **AMOCAN Premium Singapore Rendang Sauce** contains 300g of concentrated sauce and is delicious when cooked with beef, chicken or lamb.

Where available: AMOCAN and other Amoy Canning products can be found in Asia, Europe and the USA.

traditional kampong rendang

Preparation time: 45 minutes   Cooking time: 1 - 3 hours   To serve: 6

Ingredients: 1 chicken cut into pieces or 800g stewing beef, cut into 1cm slices • 3 cups thick coconut cream or freshly squeezed coconut cream from 2 coconuts • 2 tbsp vegetable oil • 1 - $1^1/_2$ tsp salt • 2 - 4 tsp sugar • 1 stalk lemon grass, crushed • 3 kaffir lime leaves (Daun Limau Purut) • 3 Turmeric leaves

Spice mixture: 5 candlenuts, washed and drained • 3 fresh chillies, stalks removed and cut into large pieces • 5 dried chillies soaked till soft in hot water • 150g shallots, peeled and roughly sliced • 1 tsp Belachan (shrimp paste) • 1 tbsp coriander powder

Method: Grind the spice mixture till fine in a food processor or pound in a pestle and mortar till you get a smooth paste. Mix all the ingredients including the spice mixture in a saucepan and bring to the boil. Simmer till the gravy thickens and the meat tender. Remove the lemon grass and the leaves. Serve with rice.

*The refreshing flavour of lemon juice complements
the sweet and creamy texture well to create the
ever popular lemon tart. Enjoy our novel
interpretation of this well-loved dessert.*

Lemon Tart

Preparation time: 10 minutes   Cooking time: Nil   To serve: 4

6 - 7 tbsp **ONG's Lemon Sauce** • 250g Cream Cheese • 1 - 2 tbsp icing sugar • 4 baked single portion pastry tart shells • candied lemon peel • a mixture of berries and fruits

Mix **ONG's Lemon Sauce**, cream cheese and icing sugar with an electric cake mixer on low speed for 10 to 15 seconds till smooth. Pipe the lemon sauce mixture onto the pastry tart shells and serve with a garnish of candied lemon peel, berries and fresh fruits. The Lemon Tart can be chilled in the fridge.

Food notes: ONG's Lemon Sauce comes in bottles of 255g. Lemon Sauce is part of a Chinese chef's culinary arsenal and has a texture much like lemon curd.

Where available: ONG's Lemon Sauce and other Bachun products can be found in Africa, the Asia Pacific, Europe and the USA.

traditional lemon curd tarts

Preparation time: 1 hour   Cooking time: 25 minutes   Cooling time: 1 hour   To serve: 4 - 6

Ingredients: 2 cups plain flour • 2 tbsp icing sugar • 180g butter, slightly softened • 1 egg yolk • 2 tbsp ice water • 150 - 200g cream cheese • lemon curd

Ingredients for lemon curd: 1 cup sugar • 2 tsp finely shredded lemon peel • 1 cup lemon juice • 3 tbsp firm butter, cut into small pieces • 3 eggs, slightly beaten

Method: Sift flour and icing sugar into a mixing bowl. Mix in butter till you get a breadcrumb texture. Add egg yolk and ice water and mix to a firm, pliable dough. Cover and store in the fridge for 30 minutes. Roll pastry thinly, cut into circles and line the insides of tart moulds. Bake at 180 degrees Celsius for 12 minutes till cooked. Cool. Cook lemon curd ingredients in a pot over low heat for 8 minutes till mixture thickens. Cool, beat with cream cheese and pipe into the tart shells.

Thin-skinned Thai limes, lemons and small limes called Limau Kesturi in Malay, clockwise from bottom left

new ideas

ONG's Lemon Sauce is a delicious alternative to lemon curd and can be used in many ways. It is thick enough to be served as jam on buttered bread and can also be mixed into cake batter to make Lemon Cake. Lemon sauce is usually served with savoury dishes like deep-fried Fillet of Fish in Batter or with fried Bread Crumb Coated Chicken Cutlet.

Speedy Chocolate Mousse

Preparation time: 5 minutes   Cooking time: Nil   To serve: 5 - 6

500g Mascarpone cheese • 200g pure cream • 4 - 5 sachets **MacChocolate 3-in-1 chocolate** • 5 - 6 Singapore Kueh Bolu sponge biscuits or 5 - 6 ladyfinger biscuits • 6 - 8 fresh cherries, halved, seeds discarded

Keep Mascarpone cheese and cream refrigerated at 5 degrees Celsius before mixing. Beat cheese, cream and contents of the 5 sachets of **MacChocolate 3-in-1 chocolate** with cake mixer on low speed for 1 minute till all the sugar in MacChocolate is dissolved. Pipe 3 to 4 tablespoons into a tall cocktail glass, put 1 Kueh Bolu or ladyfinger biscuit in the centre of the glass, add more of the chocolate mousse and top with cherries.

Food notes: MacChocolate comes in sachets of 25g each and there are 10 sachets in 1 box. This is a 3-in-1 chocolate mix which contains sugar and creamer along with the cocoa powder.

Where available: MacChocolate and other Food Empire products can be found in Central Asia, Eastern Europe and Russia.

traditional chocolate mousse classic

Preparation time: 30 minutes   Cooking time: 4 - 6 minutes   To serve: 4

Ingredients: 2 eggs • 2 - 3 tsp sugar • 200ml whipping cream • 150g dark chocolate

Method: Separate the egg yolks and white, and beat the egg white with sugar till stiff. In a separate mixing bowl whip the cream till stiff. Melt chocolate in a double boiler. If you do not have a double boiler, put the chocolate into a small saucepan over a larger saucepan of boiling water to melt the chocolate. Please note that chocolate burns easily when it comes into contact with direct heat. Quickly pour the melted chocolate into the egg yolk mixture, whipping constantly so that the yolks do not cook. Before the chocolate cools down completely, stir in about half of the whipped cream with a wooden spoon. Stir in half of the egg white, followed by the rest of the whipped cream and then add the rest of the egg white. Spoon mousse into 4 cocktail glasses and chill for at least 1 hour in the fridge before serving.

Cookie cutter and jelly moulds

Chocolate mousse is a popular classical French dessert and when served with cookies and cherries, makes for a delightful end to a meal.

new ideas

MacChocolate 3-in-1 chocolate can also be used to make cookies. Leave out sugar from the cookie recipe, and add MacChocolate powder to the biscuit dough.

freshly-ground coffee beans coffee jelly

Preparation time: 20 minutes   Cooking time: 15 minutes   To serve: 4

Ingredients: $3^1/_2$ cups water • 8 tbsp freshly ground coffee beans • 4 - 6 tsp gelatine powder • $^1/_4$ cup evaporated milk • 1 cup cream • 1 cup sugar syrup

Method: Make fresh coffee in a coffee machine or with a percolator, makes about 3 cups. Mix $^1/_2$ cup of hot coffee with gelatine powder, stir well to dissolve completely. Add the rest of the hot coffee. Put $1^1/_2$ cups coffee into a separate container and mix with the evaporated milk. Fill half a cocktail glass with black coffee jelly and chill in the fridge till set. Top with the white coffee jelly and chill till set. Serve with fresh cream and sugar syrup.

Coffee beans

new ideas

> **CAFÉ 21 Unsweetened White Coffee** is more than just a beverage. It can be made into a dessert, be added to batter for cake and can even be whipped into a coffee sauce for ice cream.

Coffee Jelly

Preparation time: 15 minutes   Chilling time: 2 - 3 hours   To serve: 2

1 sachet **CAFÉ 21 Unsweetened White Coffee** instant coffee • 1 sachet GOLD ROAST Kopi-O or GOLD ROAST Kopi-O Kosong (without sugar) • 300ml boiling hot water • 3 - 4 tsp gelatine • $^1/_2$ cup fresh cream • 2 - 3 tbsp sugar syrup, optional

Add 1 sachet **CAFÉ 21 Unsweetened White Coffee** instant coffee to 150ml boiling water. Use 3 tablespoons to mix with $1^1/_2$ to 2 tsp powdered gelatine (you can adjust the amount according on how firm you like the jelly to be). When the gelatine has dissolved, add the rest of the coffee. Dissolve the rest of the gelatine in 50ml boiling water. Mix remaining 100ml boiling water with GOLD ROAST Kopi-O or GOLD ROAST Kopi-O Kosong bags in another cup. Remove the coffee bag after 4 minutes and add the gelatine mixture. Pour the GOLD ROAST Kopi-O Kosong coffee mixture into 2 wine glasses and put in the fridge to set. When the jelly is set, top with the **CAFÉ 21 Unsweetened White Coffee** jelly mixture and put in the fridge to set. Serve with a topping of fresh cream and with sugar syrup on the side.

Food notes: **CAFÉ 21 Unsweetened White Coffee** instant coffee and GOLD ROAST Kopi-O Kosong come in packs of 30 and 20 sachets each. Kopi-O is ground coffee beans with a unique Singapore coffee flavour.

Where available: CAFÉ 21 Unsweetened White Coffee and other Viz Branz products can be found in China, Eastern Europe, Indochina, Japan, the Middle East, Southeast Asia and the USA.

Coffee desserts are an added bonus for coffee lovers.
Coffee Jelly gives that extra kick at the end
of a delicious meal.

During the cold winter months, rich foods, hot desserts and herbal tonics warm the body and soul as you sit by the fireplace enjoying intimate moments indoors with your family and friends.

Winter...

home-made marinade for chicken wings

Preparation time: 20 minutes   Cooking time: Nil   To serve: 10 chicken wings

Ingredients: 50g young ginger, pounded and squeezed for juice • 1 spring onion plant, washed and lightly crushed • 3 tbsp oyster sauce • 3½ tbsp Chinese yellow wine or sweet or dry sherry • 2 - 3 tbsp honey • ½ tsp salt, optional • 1 tsp dark soya sauce • 3 tbsp plain flour • 2 tsp sesame oil

Method: Mix all ingredients, adding sesame oil last. Use as a marinade for all kinds of meats and seafood.

Kitchen tip: For a really crispy effect, let the fried chicken wings cool down, heat the oil again till it is very hot, and deep fry the chicken wings a second time for about 30 seconds. Drain at once. With this method, you can prepare the wings a few hours ahead of serving, up to a day ahead. Let the wings cool after the first fry, keep in the fridge and then deep fry a second time just before serving. The first fry cooks the meat thoroughly, and the second crisps the outside.

Honey

new ideas

Replace chicken wings with de-boned chicken thighs and after deep frying in **SUNBEAM Sunflower Oil**, slice the meat and use it to make Chicken Honey Soy Sandwich.

Fried Chicken Wings

Preparation time: 10 minutes   Marinating time: 30 minutes
Cooking time: 7 - 9 minutes   To serve: 2 - 3

10 chicken wings weighing 850g • ¾ cup ONG'S Honey Soy Marinade or PRIMA TASTE Black Pepper Sauce or MY MUM'S Curry Sauce • ¼ tsp fine salt • ½ tsp freshly ground black pepper • 4 cloves garlic, peeled, chopped till fine • 1 cup plain flour • 5 cups **SUNBEAM Sunflower Oil**

Wash wings, pat dry with paper towels. Add ONG's Honey Soy Marinade, salt, pepper and garlic and leave for 2 hours in the fridge. Toss wings in flour. Heat the **SUNBEAM Sunflower Oil** over high heat for 4 to 5 minutes. A test for the oil's readiness is when a piece of bread sizzles in it immediately and rises to the surface. Add floured wings and deep fry over high heat for 4 minutes on one side. Turn the wings over and continue to fry till golden brown. Drain on paper towels. Serve with chilli sauce.

Food notes: SUNBEAM Sunflower Oil is conveniently packed in 1 litre or 2 kg plastic bottles.

Where available: SUNBEAM Sunflower Oil and other Sime Darby products can be found in Africa, Asia and the Middle East.

Fried chicken wings are a must-have at any Singapore party, enjoyed by both children and adults. The special taste and texture is brought out by the delicious soy sauce marinade, honey and good quality oil as well as the double frying technique to achieve golden crispiness.

traditional mother's roti prata

Preparation time: 1 hour   Resting time: 6 hours   Cooking time: 15 minutes   To serve: 12 - 15

Ingredients: 1 cup + 1 tbsp water • 1½ tbsp sugar • 1 tsp fine salt • 100g ghee (clarified butter) • 500g plain flour, sifted • 3 - 4 tbsp vegetable oil

Method: Mix 1 cup water, sugar, salt and 40g ghee, stir and add to sifted flour. Knead till dough is soft and smooth, and add more water if dough is too hard. Let dough rest for 20 minutes, shape into 50g balls, coat with remaining ghee, cover and leave for 6 hours. Flatten dough on a greased surface and then stretch and toss in the air till dough is paper thin. Fold sides in to form a square. Alternatively, roll the dough till paper thin before folding. Fry both sides till golden brown on a hot, oiled griddle.

new ideas

SPRING HOME Roti Paratha (also known as Roti Prata) can be used as a pastry wrap to wrap a variety of fillings – including Beef Rendang, Chicken Teriyaki with vegetables, sweet Fruit and Nut Compote, even Chilli Prawns. It can also be served in place of croissants with butter and jam for breakfast or for afternoon tea. Best of all, you can create a Paratha Stack or Bouquet with a wide variety of fillings made from Tasty Singapore products!

Crispy Paratha Bread with Vegetarian Curry

Preparation time: 2 minutes   Cooking time: 6 minutes   To serve: 4

8 **SPRING HOME Roti Paratha** • 2 tbsp vegetable oil, optional • 2 cans CIXIN Mock Chicken Vegetarian Curry

Heat 2 teaspoons vegetable oil and fry each of the frozen **SPRING HOME Roti Paratha** on both sides till it is puffed up, crispy and browned. Remove and put aside. Alternatively, you can fry without any oil for a healthier version. The frozen Roti Paratha can also be baked in a pre-heated oven at 200 degrees Celsius for 5 to 6 minutes till fluffy and golden brown. Do not de-frost the Roti Paratha. Heat CIXIN Mock Chicken Vegetarian Curry in a pot and serve with Roti Paratha.

Food notes: SPRING HOME Roti Paratha comes in packets of 5 or in family packs of 20. Each frozen Roti Paratha weighs about 70g.

Where available: SPRING HOME and other Tee Yih Jia products can be found in Asia, Canada, Europe, the Middle East and the USA.

Roti Paratha is one of Singapore's most well-loved foods from our Indian Muslim culinary tradition. It can be best described as an Indian puff pastry and is popular as an all-day favourite! It is usually served with curry or a sprinkling of sugar. Modern versions see fillings such as cheese, chocolate and even jam in the Roti Paratha.

Nature's harvest of roots and herbs has
featured prominently in China's wellness
practices for over 4,000 years. Their benefits
are best extracted when double boiled or
steamed to create a clear, rich broth.

Ginseng Tonic Soup

Preparation time: 10 minutes   Cooking time: 40 minutes   To serve: 2

1 can **AMOCAN Ginseng Chicken Tonic Soup** • 1 can water • 2 chicken legs, washed, patted dry with paper towels

Method: Drain the broth from the can of **AMOCAN Ginseng Chicken Tonic Soup** into a medium sized bowl and put the ginseng root and all the herbs into another. Add a can of water to the broth. Add chicken legs. Put the bowl of chicken and broth on a metal stand in a large pot or wok. Add enough water in the wok to just touch the bottom of the bowl. Cover the wok with its lid and turn on high heat. When the water in the wok boils, lower the heat to medium and steam for 40 minutes till the chicken is tender. You can steam for a longer time if desired. 20 minutes before it is done, add the herbs to the bowl of broth and stir in well. Serve as a delicious tonic soup on a cold winter night.

Food notes: Each can of **AMOCAN Ginseng Chicken Tonic Soup** contains 425g of broth and herbs. The herbs include Ginseng, Fuctus Lycii, Pochymacocos Fries, Polyganatum Officinale, Radis Codonopsitis and Red Dates.

Where available: AMOCAN and other Amoy Canning products can be found in Asia, Europe and the USA.

traditional mother's herb and ginseng soup

Preparation time: 20 minutes   Cooking time: 3 hours   To serve: 4

Ingredients: 1 dried Ginseng root • 8g dried Angelia Sinenisi roots • 18g Radis Codonopsis • 15g Dioscoreae • 6g Astragalus • 8g Ligusticum Chuanxiong Hort • 15g Polyganatum Odoratum • 18g Lycium Chinense (dried medlar) • 6 - 8 dried red dates • 1 whole spring chicken or 4 chicken legs, cleaned and dried • 4 - 5 cups water • 1/2 tsp salt, optional

Method: Put all the herbs, chicken and the water in a bowl or a double boiler. Steam (see method above) or double boil for 3 hours.

Chinese herbs

new ideas

The broth in the **AMOCAN Ginseng Chicken Tonic Soup** can be mixed with 1 can of water and dissolved gelatine to create a delicate jelly. Chill jelly in the fridge till firm and cut into cubes to decorate the top of poached chicken. Alternatively, the jelly can be put into jelly moulds with cubes of cooked chicken and chilled till firm. Remove and serve as an appetiser.

Coffee Sauce with Chicken Epicure

Preparation time: 30 minutes   Cooking time: 15 minutes   To serve: 2

500g chicken thigh, with or without bone, washed and patted dry with paper towels •
1 tbsp dark soya sauce • ¼ tsp fine salt • 1 tsp sugar • 1 tbsp tapioca or cornflour •
5 cups vegetable oil • ½ bottle **KWONG CHEONG THYE Coffee Sauce** • 6 - 10 cloves
garlic, peeled and deep fried till lightly browned • 1 chilli, cut into 1 cm lengths and lightly
stir fried in oil • 1 tbsp sesame seeds, optional, lightly toasted till light golden brown

Marinate chicken in dark soya sauce, salt, sugar and tapioca flour for 30 minutes or longer.
Deep fry chicken in hot oil till it turns golden brown. Remove chicken and drain excess oil,
leaving 1 teaspoon of oil in the wok. Add the **KWONG CHEONG THYE Coffee Sauce**
and chicken and stir-fry thoroughly. Remove and serve with garlic and garnish with chilli
and a sprinkling of sesame seeds.

Food notes: KWONG CHEONG THYE Coffee Sauce comes in bottles of 230g. The coffee
sauce is also sold in 150g sachets.

Where available: KWONG CHEONG THYE products can be found in Asia, Europe, the
Middle East and the USA.

traditional home style coffee sauce with orchard fruit

Preparation time: 15 minutes   Cooking time: 10 minutes   To serve: 3 - 4

Ingredients: 50g butter • 5 - 8 fresh cherries, pitted, optional or 1 ripe peach, pitted and
finely diced • ½ cup strong coffee made from 1½ teaspoons of instant coffee powder •
3 - 4 tbsp honey • 1 tbsp Worcestershire sauce or 1 tbsp tamarind water • ¼ tsp cardamom
powder • ½ tsp cinnamon powder • ¼ tsp nutmeg powder • 1 tsp lemon or lime juice

Method: Melt butter on a low heat, sauté fruits till slightly limp, stir in coffee, honey,
Worcestershire sauce, spices and lemon juice. Bring to boil and remove from heat.

Garlic

new ideas

KWONG CHEONG THYE Coffee Sauce with its
sweet rich flavour is an ideal accompaniment to French
style Roast Duck Breast, as well as a replacement for the
orange sauce in Duck with Orange. Its flavour makes it a
great sauce for roasted game birds and venison.

Coffee Sauce is one of the new sauce flavours created by innovative chefs in deluxe Chinese kitchens to entice the taste buds of discerning epicureans. Yes, coffee is the star ingredient in the sauce.

One of the most prized dishes in the repertoire of Chinese cuisine is steamed fish. Freshly caught fish simply cooked is sublime in texture and flavour.

new ideas

TAI HUA Seafood Soy Sauce can be used to steam prawns and clams. Use 500g prawns, cut them in half along the length and lay them on a deep platter. Steam till cooked, pour TAI HUA Seafood Soy Sauce over prawns. The sauce can also be used as a seasoning to stir fry fish or vegetables.

Steamed Fish with Spring Onions and Ginger

Preparation time: 5 minutes   Cooking time: 10 - 12 minutes   To serve: 4

5 whole spring onion plants (scallions), roots removed, washed and dried • 800g cod fillet or any white fish fillet, cut into 4 pieces • 2 tbsp SUNBEAM Sunflower Oil • 20g ginger, finely shredded • 4 tbsp **TAI HUA Seafood Soy Sauce** • 1 cup water

Blanch 4 spring onion plants in hot water for 10 seconds till the colour changes. Drain at once and put in an ice water bath. When cold, drain and pat dry. Arrange one plant in a circle on each dinner plate. In a separate large platter, steam fish for 6 to 8 minutes till cooked. Arrange a piece of fish on top of the spring onions on each plate. Fry the remaining plant of spring onion and ginger in 2 tablespoons oil for 30 seconds till fragrant. Add **TAI HUA Seafood Soy Sauce** and 1 cup water and bring to boil. Turn off heat. Remove spring onion and ginger from sauce and pour sauce over fish.

Food notes: TAI HUA specialises in producing soya sauce and their Seafood Soy Sauce is an ideal balance of soya and seasoning ingredients to create the perfect Chinese steamed fish. Each bottle contains 305ml of sauce.

Where available: TAI HUA food products can be found in the Asia Pacific, Europe, Canada, the Middle East and the USA.

traditional classical cantonese steamed fish

Preparation time: 20 minutes   Cooking time: 10 - 12 minutes   Serves: 2 - 3

Ingredients: 40g ginger • 1 cup + 4 tbsp water • 2 tbsp light soya sauce • 1/2 tsp sugar • 100g spring onions • 500g fillet of cod or any white fish • 2 tbsp vegetable oil • 1 tbsp Chinese yellow wine or sweet sherry

Method: Pound or grind ginger. Add 1 cup of water. Squeeze and discard the liquid as it will be too strong for the delicacy of the fish. Add 4 tablespoons water and squeeze for juice. This time keep the juice and add light soya sauce and sugar. Cut the spring onion plants in half and lay 1/3 of the spring onions on a long plate. Put the fish on top and add the remaining spring onions around and on top of the fish. Pour the sauce over the top and steam the fish over high heat for about 6 to 8 minutes till the fish is cooked. In the meantime, heat oil in a small saucepan, add wine and let it sizzle gently for 3 to 4 seconds and pour over the steamed fish. Serve immediately.

Fresh ginger

traditional braised teochew duck

Preparation time: 20 minutes   Cooking time: 1½ - 2 hours   To serve: 4 persons as a main dish

Ingredients: 1 large duck, weighing between 1½ - 2 kg • 20 cloves garlic • 50g Lengkuas (Galangal, also known as blue ginger) • 4 tbsp sugar • 1 cup dark soya sauce • 2 litres water • 1 piece of cinnamon stick, about 10 cm length • 5 dried cloves • 1 star anise

Method: Prepare duck for cooking (see recipe below). Crush cloves of garlic and leave them whole. Crush the piece of Lengkuas and keep aside. Heat wok and add the sugar. Let the sugar melt and caramelise on medium heat and then add the soya sauce, garlic, Lengkuas, water, cinnamon stick, cloves and star anise. Bring to the boil. Add the duck, breast side down and bring to the boil again. Detailed instructions in recipe below.

Cinnamon sticks

new ideas

TAI HUA Chinese Braising Sauce is a delicious rich broth that brings out the flavours of strong tasting meats. It is ideal for braising beef shin, oxtail, game poultry and game meats like venison.

Braised Duck with Spiced Tofu

Preparation time: 10 minutes   Cooking time: 1½ - 2 hours
To serve: 4 as a main dish

1 duck weighing 1½ - 2kg • 20 cloves garlic • 1 bottle **TAI HUA Chinese Braising Sauce** • 2 litres water • 1 packet (270g) UNICURD Five Spice Braised Tofu

Wash duck and pat dry. Cut off buttocks. Crush each clove of garlic with the back of a cleaver or in a pestle and mortar to break open the skin and to split open the garlic. Boil **TAI HUA Chinese Braising Sauce** in a large wok with the water and garlic. Add duck, breast side downwards. Bring to the boil again over high heat. Turn heat to medium and simmer for 40 minutes. Scoop the sauce over the duck every 10 mins to colour the skin. After 40 minutes, gently turn the duck over and cook the back of the duck for another 20 to 30 minutes till tender. Turn the duck over again and boil for a further 10 minutes. Test for tenderness by driving a skewer into the thick part of the thigh and if the skewer goes in easily, the meat is tender. Remove from the sauce. Allow to cool. Remove the meat from the bones and slice thinly. Serve with slices of cold UNICURD Five Spice Braised Tofu.

Food notes: TAI HUA Chinese Braising Sauce comes in 305ml bottles. This sauce is ideal for braising pork, tofu and hard-boiled eggs.

Where available: TAI HUA food products can be found in the Asia Pacific, Canada, Europe, the Middle East and the USA.

Duck is a prized meat in Chinese cooking and slow braising in soya sauce and garlic presents a great tasting dish.

traditional home-made glutinous rice balls in ginger broth

Preparation time: 1 hour   Cooking time: 35 minutes   To serve: 6 - 10

Ingredients for rice balls: 350g glutinous rice flour • 120g rice flour • 1³/₄ cups water • 200g toasted peanuts, ground till fine • 100 - 150g sugar, depending on your preference • 1 tbsp water to bind the mixture

Method: Sift and knead both flours with 1³/₄ cups hot water to form a smooth shiny dough. Cover and keep aside. Mix the ground peanuts with sugar and 1 tablespoon of water. Press the peanut mix to form a firm mix. Divide the dough and peanut mix into 30 portions and roll each into balls. Make a small dent in the centre of each dough ball and put 1 ball of peanut mix into it. Pull the dough to enclose the peanut mix totally and roll to form a round dumpling. Boil dumplings in a pot of water till they float to the surface, remove with a sieve and transfer to the pot of ginger broth. Serve 4 to 5 dumplings per person in a bowl of ginger broth.

Ingredients for ginger broth: 2 litres water • 4 pandan leaves, optional • 200g unpeeled ginger, washed and crushed to break up the ginger • 300g sugar or rock sugar

Method: Place water on high heat and add pandan leaves, ginger and sugar. Boil for 20 to 30 minutes till the water has the ginger flavour. Remove pandan leaves. Serve with the glutinous rice balls.

Raw peanuts with skin

Ginger Broth with Glutinous Rice Balls

Preparation time: 5 minutes   Cooking time: 10 minutes   To serve: 3

3 sachets **GOLD KILI Instant Ginger Drink** • 1 packet SPRING HOME Glutinous Rice Balls (10 balls weighing a total of 200g in a packet) with Yam, Black Sesame Seed or Red Bean filling • 3 cups boiling water

Add frozen SPRING HOME Glutinous Rice Balls to boiling water and boil till the balls float to the surface. In the meantime, in each serving bowl stir the contents of 1 packet of **GOLD KILI Instant Ginger Drink** with 1 cup of boiling water. Put 3 glutinous rice balls into each bowl and serve immediately as a heart-warming winter dessert.

Food notes: GOLD KILI Instant Ginger Drink comes in 18g sachets. Mix each sachet with 250 ml boiling water to make 1 cup of a refreshing beverage. 1 pack contains 20 sachets.

Where available: GOLD KILI products can be found in the Asia Pacific, South America and South Africa.

*Glutinous Rice Balls celebrate the winter solstice
in China; the longest night signals the start
of spring when days get increasingly longer and
new life emerges from the earth.*

*new
ideas*

GOLD KILI Instant Ginger Drink is usually
served as a refreshing beverage. A creative way
of using it results in shortened cooking time for one
of the classic sweet broths of Chinese cuisine – ginger
broth. You can also lightly poach slices of sweet
potato in GOLD KILI Instant Ginger Drink.

Black glutinous rice is highly nutritious and is a favoured dessert in Singapore. The Pulot Hitam porridge, served hot or cold, brings a wonderful end to a meal. It is also ideal as a cold weather treat!

Pulot Hitam

Preparation time: Nil   Cooking time: 3 minutes   To serve: 1

1 pouch of **MY MUM'S Pulot Hitam** • 2 tbsp coconut cream

Put the pouch of **MY MUM'S Pulot Hitam** into a pot of boiling water for 3 to 5 minutes to heat up. Cut open the pouch and serve. MY MUM'S Pulot Hitam is made with coconut cream, but for a richer flavour, top with 2 tablespoons of coconut cream.

Food notes: Each pouch contains 250g of **MY MUM'S Pulot Hitam** and serves 1.

Where available: MY MUM'S products can be found in Europe, the Middle East and the USA.

traditional pulot hitam dessert

Preparation time: 20 minutes   Cooking time: 2 hours   To serve: 6

Ingredients: 2 peeled grated coconuts, squeezed for milk (do not add water) or 1$\frac{1}{2}$ cups canned coconut cream • $\frac{1}{2}$ tsp salt • 200g black glutinous rice or Pulot Hitam • 2$\frac{1}{2}$ litres water • 4 pandan leaves, washed and tied into a bundle • 200g Gula Melaka (palm sugar), melted in 1 cup water and strained • 2 tbsp sugar

Method: Mix coconut milk with $\frac{1}{4}$ teaspoon salt and set it aside in the fridge. Wash black glutinous rice thoroughly and drain. Put black glutinous rice, 2$\frac{1}{2}$ litres water and pandan leave bundle into a large pot and bring to boil over high heat. Turn heat down to medium low and simmer for 1$\frac{1}{2}$ hours, stirring continuously to prevent the mixture from sticking to the bottom of the pot. Leave the pot partly uncovered so that it will not boil over. Add Gula Melaka mixture and continue to boil for 20 minutes or till the porridge is very thick. Add extra sugar to taste. Add the rest of the salt. Pour in the coconut milk and continue to stir till it boils. Serve hot or chilled. Dessert needs to cool completely before being refrigerated.

Coconut and pulot hitam

new ideas

MY MUM'S Pulot Hitam porridge can be turned into a delicious pudding by adding dissolved gelatine to the cooked porridge mixture. Pour into jelly moulds and chill. Once set, remove from the mould and serve with coconut cream for a mouth-watering dessert.

Winter Pau Medley

Preparation time: Nil   Cooking time: 15 - 18 minutes   To serve: 4

4 **KONG GUAN Mini Sweet Corn Pau** (25g each) • 4 **KONG GUAN Mini Yam Pau** (25g each) • 4 **KONG GUAN Mini Lian Yong Pau** (25g each)

The **KONG GUAN Mini Paus** are to be kept frozen. Steam the frozen paus for about 15 to 18 minutes on medium heat till the paus are piping hot all through to the centre. Serve at once as a warm winter dessert. Lian Yong is the Chinese name for lotus seed paste.

Food notes: Each packet of frozen **KONG GUAN Mini Paus** weighs 225g and contains 9 paus.

Where available: KONG GUAN products can be found in Asia, Australia, Europe and South Africa.

steamed buns with yam (taro) stuffing

Preparation time: 50 minutes   Cooking time: 40 minutes (including cooking the yam paste)
Proofing time: 2 hours   To serve: 6 - 8

Ingredients for dough: 1 tsp active dry yeast • 1/4 cup lukewarm water • 1 - 2 tbsp sugar • 1 - 1 1/2 cups lukewarm water • 3 1/2 cups plain flour or all-purpose flour • 1 1/2 tbsp vegetable oil • 1 tsp baking powder

Method: Stir and dissolve yeast and sugar in 1/4 cup water. Leave for 5 minutes till yeast bubbles. Add 1 cup lukewarm water. Add yeast mixture to flour and oil and knead into dough, sprinkle more water if dough is too firm. Knead for 10 minutes, cover, and leave in a warm place for 2 hours till doubled in volume. Punch dough, sprinkle baking powder on it and knead for 3 minutes. Make 30 portions, fill each portion with yam paste, pinching ends together to enclose yam completely. Allow to sit for 15 minutes. Steam till cooked.

Ingredients for yam paste: 600g yam, peeled • 1 cup (200g) fine sugar • 2 - 3 pandan leaves, optional

Method: Cut yam into small cubes and steam for about 5 to 6 minutes till cooked. Mash well. Put into a pot with the sugar and pandan leaves and cook, stirring constantly for about 15 to 20 minutes till the sugar has dissolved and the paste is smooth and shiny. Cool and store in the fridge.

Yam, which is also known as taro

Steamed buns called paus are delicious bite sized treats that can be eaten as part of a main meal, dessert or snack. They can be filled with meat and seafood or contain sweet pastes of yam, corn or red beans.

new ideas

KONG GUAN is an established name in frozen dim sum and paus. Dim sum items not only make great snacks, they can also be part of an appetiser, main course or dessert menu item. KONG GUAN's Gyoza for example, can be served with noodles or in soups.

Tasty Singapore Brand Ambassadors

Through the recipes in this book, one can easily identify the different tastes and experiences found in Singapore's culinary landscape. With this passion for food, it is easy to understand why Singapore's Tasty Singapore food identity is unique and distinctive.

To complement these delicious recipes, the following pages expand the Tasty Singapore personality through profiles of the Tasty Singapore brand ambassadors in the food manufacturing sector. Each has built up a wide range of processed food offerings that have leveraged the Tasty Singapore brand to gain international recognition for their products.

Amoy Canning Corporation
Preserving and Sharing an Asian Heritage

Since its incorporation in 1951 in Singapore, Amoy Canning has grown into a respected, pace-setting food manufacturer with its high quality and safety standards, and manufacturing and branding excellence.

Marketed under the Amocan brand, the company's products, prepared by trained chefs using the finest ingredients, have attained international recognition and are reflective of Singapore's culture and heritage. The company was the first to market Asian curries and local gravy and sauce favourites in a can, and has recently produced a range of healthy vegetarian products. Its extensive range of canned foods, including preserved vegetables and condiments, sauces and curry mixes, drinks and tonic soups, evidences its innovative manufacturing and packaging processes. The company has even developed a range of chicken tonic soups that is cooked in the can itself to ensure minimal loss of flavour and herb essence.

The convenience and authentic taste of Amocan products has earned them local and international popularity, with products found in many key markets. The company continues to seek out international partnerships with their distributors in Asia, USA and Europe to ensure maximum exposure for its products.

"Amoy Canning engages in continuous product development and innovation to ensure our products are of the highest standards and cater to the taste profiles of each market we are in," says Mr George Huang, Managing Director of Amoy Canning. "We are very proud of what the brand stands for."

Amoy Canning Corporation (Singapore) Ltd
23 Chin Bee Avenue
Singapore 619943
+ 65 6261 2311 tel
+ 65 6261 2800 fax
amoycanning@amocan.com
www.amocan.com
Tasty Singapore-endorsed brands: AMOCAN, CiXin Vegetarian

Bachun Food Industries
A Passion for Taste

Since its incorporation in 1976, Bachun has made a name for itself in the local wholesale market for cooking sauces and marinades. Its distinction lies in its adaptability to fast-changing food trends and taste profiles, developing products to ensure its customers adapt with minimal fuss. Its signature brands, Ong's and Bachun, serve top quality, authentic local sauces and condiments, along with a range of fusion marinades and sauces to cater to changing food trends.

To address a growing focus on Western markets with their lighter, sweeter palates, Bachun has developed a range of premium syrups to add to coffee, tea, ice cream, cakes and other desserts, under its new brand D'Vinz. Derived from the phrase "delicious and very 'in'", D'Vinz plans to introduce more new products including other gourmet syrups and a healthier range of bread spreads.

Bachun exports close to 80% of its products to Australia, New Zealand, Africa, South Asia, the USA and Europe. Almost half of their exports are catered to major food manufacturers as part of Bachun's contract manufacturing activities. In each market, the company retails its products through major distributors.

"Product development is an ongoing process for us," says Mr Ong Chun Wan, Business Development Manager for Bachun. "We are constantly innovating so that we can market new products to keep us competitive, while at the same time, add to the strength of our product offering. Our diversification to include a western-style approach to cooking will complement the strong Asian focus that we already adopt, and give our customers more choice in terms of flavours."

Bachun Food Industries (Pte) Ltd
17 Tuas Bay Walk
Singapore 637761
+ 65 6861 0518 tel
+ 65 6861 1451 fax
enquiry@bachun.com or bachunfd@pacific.net.sg
www.bachun.com
Tasty Singapore-endorsed brands: D'Vinz, Ong's

Chye Choon Foods
Poised to Shine on the World Stage

From its inception as a small family business in the late 1950s, Chye Choon's mission has been to provide wholesome and good quality foods at reasonable prices to satisfy all of its customers' needs. The company has since grown into a well-recognised leading manufacturer of rice vermicelli and rice noodles. Chye Choon's diversified product range also includes various types of imported rice, food starches, flour, sugar and other staple consumables for both retail and institutional customers. The list has grown steadily over the years in tandem with Chye Choon's marketability at home and abroad, and reflects the pride that the veteran food manufacturer and supplier takes in its ability to understand its customers' needs.

Product development is a key element of Chye Choon's business model, especially for its key Gold Leaf and Peacock brands. As part of its long-term direction to globalise its market presence, the company has created an innovative rice vermicelli range under its Peacock brand called "Quick Meals". These deliciously hearty noodles - each packet a whole meal by itself - come with fresh ready-made gravies in retort pouches to render the product the ultimate instant food. These are available in various Southeast Asian flavours, including Singapore Style Curry Chicken, Singapore Style Nonya Laksa, Singapore Style Satay Bee Hoon, Singapore Style Mee Siam, Malaysian Style Ayam Soto, Thai Style Tom Yam Rice Vermicelli, Malaysian Style Paneang (Dried Shrimp) Curry and Thai Style Green Curry Rice Vermicelli.

In recent years, Singaporeans have become more vigilant with their diet. Mirroring this positive development, Chye Choon spares little effort to ensure its recipes adhere to the Health Promotion Board's "Healthier Choice" guidelines. Among its array of options targeted at the more health-conscious, is a rice vermicelli made from pure brown rice, a good source of fibre and protein. At the same time, it strenuously shuns the use of MSG or preservatives in any of its products.

Today, Chye Choon enjoys a broad client base within the food arena and markets its products through a variety of distribution channels. "We operate under the business philosophy to continuously better ourselves and grow with our customers," says Mr Jimmy Soh, Managing Director of Chye Choon. "We are currently selling our products through distributors in Jakarta, Shanghai, Manila, New York, Vancouver, and Sydney. We are also working to build our markets in Europe and the USA because these areas present great opportunities for our products. Using these strategies, we envision growing to become a highly respected global food company within the next six years."

Chye Choon stays abreast of the latest food trends and tastes through frequent interactions with, and feedback from, its customers. It regularly attends international food shows to gain a better insight into the various markets where it distributes its products, and to catch up with new standards in food processing. This has helped the company to stay competitive with tasty products, high customer service standards and more importantly, the consistently great quality its customers have come to love and trust.

Chye Choon Foods Private Limited
34 Defu Lane 3
Singapore 539451
+ 65 6283 5470 tel
+ 65 6285 6519 fax
jimmy@chyechoon.com.sg
www.chyechoon.com.sg
Tasty Singapore-endorsed brands: PEACOCK BRAND

Country Foods
Ingredients That Don't Come Any Fresher

As a producer and distributor of fresh-cut vegetables, fruit and meat, whose clients include quick service restaurants and international fast food chains, Country Foods' maxim is to delight its customers through the freshest consistency in all its product offerings. This, it measures and improves with technology, based on the perishability, variety, taste and quality of its meat and produce.

But beyond fresh-cut vegetables, fruit and meat, Country Foods also develops and distributes a range of frozen ready-to-eat Asian meals and sandwiches. Working with experienced chefs and a trained catering team, Country Foods develops these specialised meals in its highly sanitised central facility – producing healthier food options with no compromise on taste. Clients include airlines, convenient stores, tourist attractions, hospitals and medical institutions.

"To take our food processing standards to the highest quality levels, requires us to use nothing but the freshest ingredients" says Mr Alvin See, General Manager of Country Foods. "Whether we're delivering vegetables, fruit or meat, there can simply be no compromise on this. And although our convenient meal packs are frozen, we use only special freezing techniques to ensure that our products stay fresher longer and that our customers get meals that seem as if they were freshly prepared."

"With a relatively small cluster of food companies in Singapore, the Tasty Singapore platform will help consolidate individual marketing efforts into a stronger consolidated brand with a more organised marketing strategy, thereby facilitating easier entry into new and international markets."

Country Foods Pte Ltd
22 Senoko Way
Singapore 758044
+ 65 6753 4188 tel
+ 65 6752 0866 fax
enquiries@countryfoods.com.sg
www.countryfoods.com.sg
Tasty Singapore-endorsed brands: Sky D'light

Food Empire Holdings
Sharing Moments with You

Passionate about the products it develops, markets and exports, Food Empire is committed to developing strong brands to which customers will become emotionally attached. Boasting a portfolio of over 200 products, including instant beverages, frozen convenience and snack foods, and confectionery items, Food Empire markets its products to more than 50 countries around the world. The company enjoys a large market share for its instant 3-in-1 beverages in Russia, Eastern Europe and Central Asia.

Food Empire manages many well-known brands, such as MacCoffee, Klassno, MacCandy and Kracks, and capitalises on its extensive international networks, vast market knowledge and product expertise to achieve international success. Food Empire sponsors a host of events including the World Cup, motor rallies and more recently, the Tienshan mountain climbing expedition in Central Asia.

The company's belief in constant product development and innovation has earned it numerous awards for its quality standards, production excellence, product range and packaging designs. Food Empire and its MacCoffee brand have been recognised as one of the "Most Valuable Singapore Brands" and one of the "Strongest Singapore Brands" respectively.

"We are a company that is driven by passion and an entrepreneurial spirit to create excellent products for the markets. The Group continues to achieve market success with the support of its people and consumers," says Ms Daphne Wan, Marketing Communications Manager of Food Empire. "In Tasty Singapore, we are banking on the high regard Singapore has for its food standards, to help companies like us create an even stronger network of export markets that we can tap into."

Food Empire Holdings Limited
101 Geylang Lorong 23 #05-03/04
Prosper House
Singapore 388399
+ 65 6744 8911 tel
+ 65 6744 8977 fax
info@food-empire.com
www.food-empire.com
Tasty Singapore-endorsed brands: KLASSNO, MacChocolate, MacCoffee

Gan Hup Lee
An Ingrained Reverence for Rice

When you pick up a packet of Yamie Rice, you can be sure that the grains are exactly right for the flavour they're infused with. That's because Gan Hup Lee (GHL), the makers of Yamie Rice, are past masters at assessing and differentiating to the smallest detail the wide variety of rice on the market.

Yamie Rice is the latest bestseller from a company that has come of age as a major rice and oil distributor in Singapore. Since it was set up in 1949, GHL has introduced a steadily-expanding repertoire of the staple grain to suit the population's diverse tastes and cuisines.

Much of the fragrant rice that the company imports is available under its Golden Padi and Golden Star brands, both offering special-grade fragrant rice varieties of superior quality. These are imported directly from rice-growing regions in Thailand, and sold to a variety of businesses in the food and beverage trade - restaurants, canteen stallholders, hawkers and caterers. These same businesses also account for almost all the company's sales of cooking oil. GHL's product range and expertise come in handy here – most of its customers tend to specialise in similar types of food and dishes.

As GHL's general manager, Mr Dicky Yeo, puts it, "With over 55 years of experience in this business, we are able to understand and analyse the different characteristics of rice and to give customers exactly what they want. For instance, when cooking claypot rice, you want to use harder rice to absorb the flavours of the ingredients in the claypot. With porridge, new rice is best because it's softer. There's no book to teach you these things. Our late founder could pick up a handful of rice and, with his eyes closed, tell you what type of rice it was."

Inspired by demand from Singapore visitors for tastes "they enjoyed here but couldn't find back home", GHL's R&D team got together with the Singapore Polytechnic, to create a series of super-convenient flavoured rice meals. With no real cooking necessary nor additional troublesome pouches of ingredients, all that was necessary was to just heat up a packet, and sit down to a steaming plate of Hainanese Rice, Chicken Rice or Yam Rice - Singapore style. More exciting choices, including Claypot Rice, Nasi Beryani and Pineapple Rice, are being developed by the company, each, of course, perfectly matching the type of rice to flavour.

GHL takes its grains so seriously that it is one of only a few companies in the region to use the state-of-the-art *Rice Colour Sorter* as a quality control measure. The imported machine, housed at GHL's dedicated laboratory within its own new building, screens for only the best grains - anything less is discarded as unfit for sale.

HACCP-certified and designated a Healthier Choice food by the Health Promotion Board, Yamie Rice is currently available in 'Chinatown' within many cities around the world. Its Halal certification also paves the way for its entry into Muslim markets in the region.

Gan Hup Lee (1999) Pte Ltd
16 Chin Bee Avenue
GHL Building
Singapore 619939
+ 65 6741 2626 tel
+ 65 6741 0129 fax
dickyyeo@ganhuplee.com
www.ganhuplee.com
Tasty Singapore-endorsed brands: YAMIE RICE

Gold Kili Trading Enterprise
Maximum Taste and Instant Convenience

Established in 1979, Gold Kili has become a leading manufacturer and supplier of instant beverages in Singapore. Its extensive product range includes its 3-in-1 range of instant coffees, teas and cereals, premium coffee bags, instant red date beverages and a variety of green teas. Gold Kili was the first company to launch innovative products such as the instant honeyed chrysanthemum drink, instant honeyed ginger drinks, and 2-in-1 coffee bags.

To build a strong brand and cultivate brand loyalty both locally and internationally, Gold Kili employs a two-pronged approach to their branding initiatives – introducing the Qilin mascot, an animated dragon, as the company's spokesperson, and embracing a new marketing slogan, "Just Gold Kili n Water", to emphasise the convenience of its products.

The company's commitment to new product development is evident in the recently launched cafe latte series that includes milk coffees in various flavours and an instant honeyed ginger latte drink. Gold Kili also introduced two Singapore-signature coffees: Espresso Asia, the first espresso coffee bag in Singapore, and Espressccino, an espresso with the frothiness of a cappucino. Besides supplying to local supermarkets and food service channels, Gold Kili also contract manufactures its products for private label clients.

"We are still a relatively new company on the international front," says Mr Desmond Ng, Managing Director of Gold Kili. "Although we have a market presence in Asia, Europe, Canada, Australia, the USA, Africa and New Zealand, the bulk of our products is still distributed in the local market. We are always on the lookout for good international distributors who can carry and promote our products in their own markets. This is one of the areas that the Tasty Singapore brand can help us in and complement our own branding."

Gold Kili Trading Enterprise (Singapore) Pte Ltd
48 Senoko Drive
Singapore 758231
+ 65 6854 2775 tel
+ 65 6854 2558 fax
mkt@goldkili.com or query@goldkili.com
www.goldkili.com
Tasty Singapore-endorsed brands: Gold Kili

Hai's
Traditional Recipes You'll Just Love

Authentic Singapore dishes that are simple to prepare served in minutes are Hai's speciality. Their range of ready-to-cook sauces and pastes are produced with the best ingredients and spices, encompassing traditional dishes Laksa, Mee Siam and Soto, and popular favourites such Rendang and Chicken Rice.

In addition to serving local customers, the company also markets to countries like Australia, Brunei, Hong Kong and Taiwan, and has customised some of their products, including Hot Shrimp Paste and Chilli Crab Paste, to accommodate western taste palates. The versatility of its products has made it a popular choice, as it is able to be used as a steamboat soup, dipping sauce and even salad dressing pasta sauce.

To keep abreast of the latest trends and taste profiles, the company regularly carries out market research as part of its product development process. This commitment to customer satisfaction extends to its product packaging, with selected recipes on the back to help customers prepare and fully appreciate each dish.

"All the recipes we use for our sauces, pastes and seasonings are traditional favourites that have been handed down generation after generation," says Mr Lim Swee Hai, Managing Director of Hai's. "These recipes call for freshest ingredients and are prepared so that none of flavour of these time-tested favourites is lost. The delicious taste you experience with Hai's products is exactly the same as when it was enjoyed generations ago."

Hai's Pte Ltd
Blk 15 Woodlands Loop #03-02/04/05/30
Singapore 738322
+ 65 6752 8588 tel
+ 65 6758 9288 fax
enquiry@hais.com.sg
www.hais.com.sg
Tasty Singapore-endorsed brands: Hai's

Kim Hing Food Industries
Where Quality is a Prerequisite

Once synonymous with imperial cuisine and traditional remedy, bird's nest today has become more mainstream as its health benefits receive wider recognition.

The measure of good bird's nest – an oriental delicacy – is in its taste, texture, consistency, quality and preparation. With its commitment to top quality manufacturing, it is little wonder that Kim Hing's Dragon brand of bird's nest enjoys wide popularity. Its range of standard to premium products include bird's nest with varying sugar content, or combined with other health products such as ginseng and cordyceps. In addition to boxed, pre-cooked bird's nest, Dragon brand bird's nest is also available bottled and ready to drink or concentrated. Its innovative and convenient packaging ensures product quality and freshness are uncompromised and preserved. Moreover, its 'halal' certification makes its products accessible to Muslims in Kim Hing's key markets, where Dragon brand bird's nest products are sold through retail buyers, distributors and specialty shops.

"Trust in the brand usually equates to trust in our bird's nest products," says Mr Allan Tan, President of Kim Hing. "This means we have to ensure that each bottle of bird's nest sold maintains the high standards which our Dragon brand has come to be valued for. We take quality very seriously; profit at the expense of quality is not an option for us."

Having Tasty Singapore's endorsement will reinforce Kim Hing's own brand values of high safety and quality standards. At the same time, the acknowledgement of Dragon brand bird's nest as a Singapore brand serves to reinforce the positive perception of Singapore as a trusted source of high quality food.

Kim Hing Food Industries Pte Ltd
60 South Bridge Road
Singapore 058690
+ 65 6538 2288 tel
+ 65 6533 7446 fax
kimhing@singnet.com.sg or allan@dragonbrand.com.sg
www.dragonbrand.com.sg
Tasty Singapore-endorsed brands: Dragon Brand, Kim's Brand

Kong Guang Dumpling / Pau Manufacturer
Steamed to Perfection

Literally translated from Chinese as "the Source of Good Health", Kong Guan has been producing fresh and frozen steamed buns ('pau') and dumplings since 1969. It uses the best ingredients, adopts strict quality control measures and employs innovative manufacturing methods to eliminate all preservatives, reduce salt and oil content, and ensure a longer shelf life while retaining the taste and nutritional value of its products.

Kong Guan carries a wide range of Asian products, including dumplings, savoury snacks, dim sum, and a Halal range of 'pau' and satay (meat skewers) catered to the Muslim and Middle Eastern markets. In addition, the company also develops customised food products for private labels.

Deeply committed to innovation, the company introduced the hugely popular, bite-sized mini 'pau', and recently showcased an inventive new packaging that ensures microwaved 'paus' retain the texture and quality of a steamed version. This unique packaging material has won the company several accolades, including one at the 'Road to Innovation, Paris' during SIAL2004.

"Healthy, tasty and convenient – these are the pillars that have defined Kong Guan steamed buns over the years," says Ms Mona Sim, Senior Marketing Manager. "In Singapore, our customers keep coming back to us time and again because we constantly deliver the tried and tested standard in our 'pau' that they have come to expect. We are now looking to ensure that our international customers are able to enjoy the same experience."

Kong Guan Dumpling / Pau Manufacturer Pte Ltd
8 Woodlands Link
Kong Guan Industrial Building
Singapore 738738
+ 65 6776 6688 tel
+ 65 6257 0220 fax
kongguan@kongguan.com.sg
www.kongguan.com.sg
Tasty Singapore-endorsed brands: Kong Guan

Kwong Cheong Thye
Taking Product Innovation to New Heights

A sauce pioneer with a century-old legacy and modern sensibilities, Kwong Cheong Thye carries a wide range of soy sauces, specialty seasoning sauces and pastes, noodles and mooncake pastes.

Its continuous product development has led to the introduction of innovations such as its Professional Chef sauce, its award-winning Coffee Sauce as well as a range of healthy alternatives including lower sodium, lower sugar, high protein and less oil variations. Even its packaging has become more eye-catching, durable and as space and weight-efficient over time.

Kwong Cheong Thye enjoys close to 90% market share for its sauces and pastes in Singapore, and is used extensively in hotels and restaurants. It also enjoys international exposure in markets such as Indonesia, China, USA, Japan, Europe and the Middle East. The company uses distributors to market its products in these regions, but also sells through retail shops in London, Amsterdam and Australia to further enhance its global presence.

"We want to constantly innovate products that consumers can use to whip up delicious restaurant-style dishes," says Mrs Alice Choo, Director of Kwong Cheong Thye. "These easy-to-cook sauces and pastes are for both household cooking and for chefs in food services or industrial kitchens. We use only the purest of ingredients in our sauces and pastes to ensure fast and efficient cooking without compromising on taste."

Kwong Cheong Thye believes that being co-branded by Tasty Singapore will enable it to specifically market products uniquely Singaporean in flavour, process and quality standards. On a group level, the company hopes that the brand equity of Tasty Singapore will help benchmark Singapore food as a premium standard on the world stage.

Kwong Cheong Thye Pte Ltd
12 Senoko Avenue
Singapore 758302
+ 65 6748 7766 tel
+ 65 6286 5948 fax
kctsoya@pacific.net.sg
www.kctsoya.com
Tasty Singapore-endorsed brands: Kwong, Kwong Cheong Thye

My Mum's Cuisine
Trustworthy Sauces

With a name that evokes the ambient scents of home cooking, My Mum's Cuisine has, unsurprisingly, acquired something of a culinary cult following in Singapore. The brand began life as a restaurant in 1995, serving a delicious fusion of popular Peranakan and Hainanese favourites based on the time-honoured recipes of its founder's mother. Since then, the brand has acquired strong competencies in sauce manufacturing and catering services as well. Today, My Mum's Cuisine also manages the Noodle Hut restaurants in Singapore.

A warm and inviting decor that harkens back to the eateries of old, friendly yet impeccable service, and most importantly, an extensive, well-loved menu; these are the attributes that have defined My Mum's Cuisine over time. In addition to time-tested evergreen dishes, the restaurant regularly unveils innovative dishes to keep its customers coming back for more of this endearing mix of past and present. Indeed, some of its newest inventions have been showcased and honoured at numerous food shows, an example being its Sambal Crab La Mien - selected as one of the Top 10 new dish creations at the Singapore Food Festival 2004.

The popularity of its menu and the need to expand its business scope has led My Mum's Cuisine to replicate the tastes of its bestselling dishes in a more portable form. As a result, its much-heralded Satay, Sambal Chilli, Curry, Sweet and Sour, Sichuan and Laksa flavours are literally going places in ready-to-cook sauces under the My Mum's label. Equally welcome is its range of ready-to-eat local desserts - Pulot Hitam, Buboh Cha Cha and Tau Suan - combining authentic tradition and convenience in a sachet.

To date, these products are marketed to many areas world-wide including Ghana, the United Kingdom, Australia, New Zealand and Japan, quite remarkable coverage considering that the overseas marketing campaign only began in 2003. The company is also pulling out the stops and taking all efforts to continue its globalisation efforts. The USA, Europe and the Middle East are definitely on the company's radar as far as its convenience foods go. There are plans to take the restaurant farther afield too.

"In the long term, we want to work with franchisees and partners in joint ventures to open more My Mum's Cuisine restaurants in markets like Moscow, Tokyo and Osaka," says Ms Diana Cheng, the company's Founder and Managing Director. Already, its collaboration with a major hotel group has borne fruit in Malaysia. A ritzy version of My Mum's Cuisine recently opened in Starhill Gallery in Kuala Lumpur, Malaysia.

Meanwhile, quality enhancement remains the overriding goal across the business. R&D has already improved the shelf life of many of its sauces and its desserts by up to 24 months without refrigeration using its special retort packaging techniques. In addition, the company is also planning to launch a new range of ready-mix complete noodle meals with such flavours as Beef Bolognaise, Chicken Garlic and Vegetarian Tomato, which customers need only to pop into a microwave and heat up to enjoy.

My Mum's Cuisine Pte Ltd
290 Orchard Road
#14-03 Paragon
Singapore 238859
+ 65 6887 5168 tel
+ 65 6734 9330 fax
diana@mymumscuisine.com
www.mymumscuisine.com
Tasty Singapore-endorsed brands: My Mum's

Owl International
Tradition in a Cup

With a strong 50-year heritage in the production of roasted and ground coffee, Owl International has grown its product offering to its current stable of eight beverage brands, each representing multiple products and packaging, catering to different tastes and target markets.

The first beverage company in Singapore to acquire the HACCP safety rating, Owl International enforces stringent quality standards in the production of its extensive products, which include roast and ground coffees, 3-in-1 coffees, teas and cereals.

Always mindful of the specific taste profiles of its target audiences in its export markets, the company offers customised products, including 'tarik' (pulled) and 'halia' (ginger) teas catered to its Middle Eastern consumers, creamer coffees to the Indian subcontinent, and spiced and herbal teas to its Western markets.

"Besides developing new products with new taste profiles and innovative packaging, we also explore creative uses for our products," says Ms Sherie Koh, Assistant General Manager of Owl International. "Our coffee, for instance, can be used to make ice cream, while our lemon tea makes a savoury lemon chicken dish. Our ultimate focus, however, is still on developing ideas and innovations to nurture and enhance traditional coffee drinking."

"In Singapore, the Owl brand has become synonymous with ground coffee powder," says Ms Jenny Lim, General Manager of Owl International. "Going forward we will continue to focus on achieving the highest quality, variety and taste for our products. Our customers would expect no less."

Owl International recently merged with Super Coffeemix, also an internationally marketed beverage company. Their combined synergies will be further enhanced by the endorsement of the Tasty Singapore brand, which will help to fast-track Owl's export into potential markets.

Owl International Pte Ltd
37 Chin Bee Crescent, Jurong Town
Singapore 619903
+ 65 6268 8100 tel
+ 65 6268 5988 fax
reachus@owl.com.sg
www.owl.com.sg
Tasty Singapore-endorsed brands: Owl

Prima Food
The Taste That's Taking on the World

Prima Food is in the business of food manufacturing, licensing and franchising. Its signature brand, Prima Taste, has earned awards and accolades for its premium quality ready-to-cook pastes and sauces.

Launched in 1999, Prima Taste's 'Best Singapore Favourites' range of main dishes, side dishes, desserts and dips offers over 30 authentic Singapore favourites, such as Laksa and Hainanese Chicken Rice, in easy-to-use, ready-to-cook pastes. Each pack comes complete with essential ingredients and condiments, ensuring a full complement of authentic, consistently delicious tastes and flavours.

Prima Taste's products, which include its 'Authentic Asia' range of versatile cooking sauces for whipping up delectable Asian-style dishes, are available in retail, foodservice and premium gift packs, marketed locally and internationally through distributors.

In 2000, Prima Food launched the Prima Taste 'True Singapore Cuisine' concept restaurants, serving authentic and delicious Singapore dishes that showcase the premium quality of Prima Taste products.

"Prima Taste products are now exported to more than 15 countries worldwide, including USA, Canada, UK, Australia, China and Japan," says Mr Lewis Cheng, General Manager of Prima Food Pte Ltd. "Our strategy to promote Singapore cuisine and Prima Taste globally is three-pronged. We have retail products for the consumers and foodservice solutions for restaurant and cafe operators. We have also launched the Prima Taste restaurant franchise in cities like San Jose, Shanghai, Perth, Manila and Jakarta so potential customers in these countries can sample Singapore food and appreciate our food heritage. As testimony to the premium quality of Prima Taste products, the restaurants themselves are viable F&B operations."

Prima Food also manages the award-winning PrimaDeli bakery chain, Singapore's first home-grown bakery franchise and longest-running food franchise. The chain boasts more than 40 bakeries in Singapore and nine in Malaysia. In addition, Prima Food manufactures a range of breads, buns and pastries in frozen dough form for foodservice operators.

Prima Food Pte Ltd
201 Keppel Road, Level 5 Office Block
Singapore 099419
+ 65 6277 6833 tel
+ 65 6277 6890 fax
sales.primataste@prima.com.sg
www.primataste.com
Tasty Singapore-endorsed brands: Prima Taste

Seng Hua Hng Foodstuff
Extra Crunchy Good-Time Snacks

Considered the ideal good-time food, Seng Hua Hng's Camel brand of nut products use only the best quality nuts sourced from the USA, New Zealand, Australia, India and China. Camel's extensive range of 40 different product lines enjoys international exposure in 14 countries, with major markets in Asia and the Middle East.

Seng Hua Hng markets its products overseas through a combination of distributors and local partners. All of them are tasked to help build brand awareness and loyalty, and have contributed to the increase in sales and enhanced marketing networks the company now enjoys. Locally, Camel nuts are distributed to every major supermarket and retail chain, and are the most popular snack of choice for major hotels, restaurants and other food service channels.

The only Singaporean nut manufacturer, with manufacturing facilities in Singapore and China, Seng Hua Hng is the clear market leader in this category. But the company continues to innovate, striving to introduce at least two new commercially viable products every year. Its latest offerings include wasabi (horseradish) peanuts, abalone macadamias, a premier nuts canister range, nonya spring rolls with authentic nonya prawn filling, and a natural cocktail mix of nuts and dried fruits.

"Our core business objectives are to nurture the bonds we have with our suppliers, distributors and partners," says Ms Poh Shih Yin, Finance Manager of Seng Hua Hng. "This is what has kept us resilient, a trait easily recognised in the Camel symbol we use to represent our products. We also have ambitions to expand into regions like South Africa and Eastern Europe, and we believe the Tasty Singapore brand can help us increase our presence there."

Seng Hua Hng Foodstuff Pte Ltd
127 Defu Lane 10
Singapore 539234
+ 65 6383 3388 tel
+ 65 6383 0689 fax
queries@camelnuts.com
www.camelnutes.com
Tasty Singapore-endorsed brands: Camel

Sime Darby Edible Products
A Well-oiled Outfit

A fully-owned subsidiary of the Sime Darby Group, Sime Darby Edible Products Limited (SDEPL) is one of Singapore's major oil refiners. With more than six decades of experience in producing edible oils, the company manages the refining and downstream processing of these oils, and operates a high-tech manufacturing plant to ensure that only the freshest and best quality edible oil products are produced. The company also specialises in customised edible oil products for individual customer requirements.

SDEPL provides a wide variety of packaging choices for its edible oils and this has endeared the company to its many customers as it is always ready to cater to their ever-changing needs and preferences. Today, SDEPL carries a wide stable of brands under its range of fine quality edible oils. These are exported worldwide under the brand names of Sunbeam, Golden Drop, La Bella, Chief, Hand, King Rooster, Vego Maza, CBC, Leila, Cook, Dairy Fresh and Spoons.

SDEPL's premium marque of cooking oils is its 'Sunbeam' brand, a range comprising pure sunflower, groundnut, canola, corn and soya oils. Sunbeam also carries a selected range of Nyonya sauces as well as flavoured instant rice products in a variety of authentic Singaporean flavours such as Hainanese Chicken Rice, Nasi Lemak and Garlic Rice.

"Quality and reliability are two extremely important factors which we emphasise," says Ms Sarah Lin, Marketing Executive of Sime Darby Edible Export Marketing. "Stringent and hygienic controls are exercised throughout our manufacturing process and our quality control team ensures that all our products meet international and contractual specifications. Although a growing list of our products has been awarded the Singapore Institute of Standards & Industrial Research (SISIR) endorsement, a hallmark for excellence in quality, we still undertake continuous research and development to improve our products."

Through forging global links with its sister companies and subsidiaries, as well as being a member of leading research and processing organisations, the company constantly keeps abreast of the latest developments in oil technology and research. SDEPL is also certified to HACCP, ISO 9001, Kosher, Halal and Healthier Choice standards, and this has certainly helped gear the company for internationalisation, increasing its global market share and opening up new international customer bases in current, new and unexplored markets.

The company also plans to extend its product offering while pursuing its top-of-agenda objective of expanding its market presence within each market it enters.

Sime Darby Edible Products Limited
255 Jalan Boon Lay
Singapore 619524
+ 65 6264 3733 tel
+ 65 6265 5129 fax
sarah@sdepl.com
www.simedarbyepl.com.sg
Tasty Singapore-endorsed brands: Sunbeam

Sin Hwa Dee Foodstuff
Innovative in Every Way

Since the 1970s, Sin Hwa Dee has been producing CHNG Kee's high-quality Chinese and Asian sauces. The company aims to become a global market leader through innovations in product development, manufacturing and marketing of its convenient and healthy food.

Besides producing oyster, soy and other basic sauces, Sin Haw Dee was the first to produce ready-to-use Laksa paste for the food service industry. Its product innovation includes line extensions of its sauces and premixes, its ready-to-use meal pastes and even gift packs for tourists to bring home a taste of Singapore. Its investments in R&D, technologically advanced equipment and facilities and fully-computerised order fulfillment mechanisms ensure high standards of efficiency and quality assurance.

The company established a unique 'Spice of Life' retail concept, partnering their retail store with an adjoining eatery featuring local favourites made from their CHNG Kee's brand of products. Sin Hwa Dee is sourcing for partners to expand this creative concept beyond its current tourist locations to other local and international retail areas. Their innovative marketing strategy includes brand communication activities such as advertising in local and foreign publications; cooking classes, workshops and seminars; international cooking competitions; and active participation in international tradeshows, and they have earned several brand awards.

Sin Hwa Dee has a presence in more than 30 countries worldwide, including USA, Europe, the Middle East, and Taiwan, and its exports continue to grow exponentially every year.

"We want people to recognise CHNG Kee's as a homegrown brand and a household name," says Ms Jocelyn Chng, Managing Director of Sin Hwa Dee. "We also want our customer, whether local or international, retail or commercial, to form a positive association with our products, and then we build on and enhance the brand experience from there."

As an ambassador of Tasty Singapore, Sin Hwa Dee is keen to bring the taste of Singapore to every corner of the world, while leveraging its own brand identity in the joint partnership to attain global prominence.

Sin Hwa Dee Foodstuff Industries Pte Ltd
No 8 Senoko South Road
CHNG Kee's Foodlink
Singapore 758095
+ 65 6755 2262 tel
+ 65 6755 6656 fax
clairechng@shdfood.com.sg
www.chngkees.com.sg
Tasty Singapore-endorsed brands: CHNG Kee's

Sin Mui Heng
A Knack for Tasty Snacks

To refer to Sin Mui Heng as simply a manufacturer of dim sum is akin to describing Mount Everest as a rather tall peak. This is because what the company produces at its six factories in Singapore, Malaysia and China is a staggering variety of over 300 assorted dim sum - a far wider range than you would find in even the most ambitious Cantonese restaurant anywhere. Today, its dim sum is sold in bulk, to supermarkets and other retailers, or as bento sets customised for private functions.

Every year, Sin Mui Heng introduces between 20 and 30 new variations on these quintessentially Chinese teahouse snacks, marketed under its three brands, 'Sin Mui Heng', 'SMH' and 'Xing Food'. Occasionally, it may create customised varieties using special ingredients like abalone, for example, at a client's request. Its prolific inventiveness simply offers proof of a company that lives and breathes innovation.

Established in 1961, Sin Mui Heng began investing heavily in its own machinery in the late 1970s and then went on to become the first food company in Southeast Asia to automate its production facilities. In due course, it achieved the methodology to mass produce frozen and chilled dim sum that retained its nutritional value, freshness and taste. It is hardly surprising then, that this family business became the first dim sum maker in Singapore to be awarded ISO 9001 certification in 2001.

The company chalked up another "first" with its foray into Halal manufacturing. The true innovation in this milestone was that the technique acquired to ensure that a change in ingredients did not compromise the authenticity of the snacks. "We do not only replace pork with chicken. It took us 10 years of research to replicate the taste and texture of the original dim sum in our Halal versions," says Mr Johnson Tay, Sin Mui Heng's Director of Operations. The move has opened up a potentially vast Muslim market to its brand of dim sum, made with only the finest and freshest ingredients to the most stringent production standards. Today, ninety percent of Sin Mui Heng's output comes from its Halal-certified factories.

Sin Mui Heng's customer base includes more than eighty percent of the hotels and caterers in Singapore. Its fare is also served to First Class airline passengers as well as at many high-level functions. Supermarkets island-wide stock many of its dim sum products including its two key bestsellers - *siew mai* and *pau*.

Because Sin Mui Heng is adamant about sacrificing the quality of its ingredients for cost effectiveness, the company is usually unwilling to engage its competitors in a price war. This means that it tends to take its dim sum products only to markets where consumers have more discerning and discriminating taste profiles. Currently, about five percent of its total production is exported to the Maldives, Canada, Australia and Brunei. The company's next stop is the Middle East, where it already gained acceptance and approval as an official food supplier for the 2006 Asian Games in Doha, Qatar.

Sin Mui Heng Food Industries Pte Ltd
3017 Bedok North Street 5
#05-06 Gourment East Kitchen
Singapore 486121
+ 65 6442 7677 tel
+ 65 6442 7577 fax
evan@smhfood.com
www.smhfood.com
Tasty Singapore-endorsed brands: Sin Mui Heng, SMH and Xing Food

Super Coffeemix
A Matter of Convenience

Established in 1987, Super Coffeemix is a leading manufacturer of instant coffee and tea beverages as well as other drinks and convenience foods. The Singapore-listed company boasts an extensive portfolio of more than 300 products distributed through a network spanning 52 countries worldwide. Its product range comprises a variety of conventional as well as specialty coffees, teas, cereals, canned drinks, instant noodles and other daily consumables such as non-dairy creamers and distilled water.

Fans of Super Coffeemix everywhere relish the ease-of-use, convenience and great taste of its myriad innovations. Awarded Pioneer Status by Singapore's Economic Development Board in 1993, the company commands strong brand and product loyalty among its customers. This is chiefly due to its commitment to ensure their enjoyment of its products regardless of their specific taste profiles. The tirelessly inventive manufacturer has also embraced innovative R&D strategies, with various product development programmes securely in place to ensure the results meet the changing tastes and preferences of its consumers. It has geared different brands and products towards particular groups with gratifying success. For example, its *Grandeur* range is targeted at busy executives while *Café Nova* appeals primarily to youths. Super Coffeemix has even developed a new *Café Nova Oligofructose with Prebiotics* to help reduce bad intestinal bacteria and aid digestion.

Super Coffeemix is in constant touch with the latest market taste trends, and regularly introduces fresh variations on its staple offerings to give its convenience-addicted customers more choice. It released close to 30 new products last year alone, including innovative 2-in-1 coffee mixes targeted at health-conscious drinkers. Among them were *Café Nova Unsweetened, Café White* and *Grandeur Coffee*, welcomed by consumers because they contain 45% fewer calories than normal coffee. The company has also introduced various other innovative products including its unique *Super Kimchi Cup Noodles*, ready-to-eat noodles which have become a hit with its customers. Besides product variations, Super Coffeemix is also exploring other areas of growth as well. It recently launched special-portion beverage cups mainly for the airline and hotel industries.

Clearly, the breadth of Super Coffeemix's customer base attests to the company's unyielding dedication to quality. "We manufacture our own coffee powder from raw green beans and non-dairy creamer," says Mr Teo Kee Bock, Managing Director of Super Coffeemix. "We are the only ASEAN company with the manufacturing capabilities to produce instant soluble coffee, cereal flakes and non-dairy creamers. To date, we have 13 manufacturing facilities across Singapore, Malaysia, China, Myanmar, Indonesia and Thailand. This enables us to ensure quality and consistency in all our products every time. This is what we strive to deliver to our customers."

Super Coffeemix has, over the years, garnered numerous awards for its products, its innovative process and especially its marketing and branding programmes. They include the prestigious Monde Selection award for its Super 3-in-1 Coffeemix as well as the Singapore Brand Award 2003, a national prize recognising the strongest local brands.

Super Coffeemix Manufacturing Limited
2 Senoko South Road
Super Industrial Building
Singapore 758096
+ 65 6753 3088 tel
+ 65 6753 7833 fax
elaine@super.com.sg
www.super.com.sg
Tasty Singapore-endorsed brands: SUPER

Tai Hua Food Industries
Where Quality is the Sauce of Life

Tai Hua's 58 years of success stems from its traditional taste and deep commitment to quality. Exporting to more than 30 countries around the globe, including the USA, Asia, the Middle East, and Europe, Tai Hua brews its soy sauces from premium natural ingredients, resulting in a pure, flavourful sauce.

Tai Hua products are present in most Singapore homes, food companies and catering operations, and are also contract manufactured for private labels. In addition to its signature soy sauces, the company produces braising sauces, ready-to-cook sauces and pastes, and distributes canned foods and fruits.

Currently ranked one of Asia's top 500 brands, Tai Hua has garnered many honours for its brand building, packaging and health food status, including the Asian Star Packaging awards and Singapore Promising Brand Award. It also received the Agri-food Veterinary Authority's Food Safety Excellence Award for attaining Grade A status 12 years in a row.

"We believe strongly that good quality is critical to building trust in a brand and to business sustainability – quality not only in our products but in every aspect of our organisation, from sourcing to sales to internationalisation," says Mr Thomas Pek, Managing Director of Tai Hua. "Singapore is a brand in itself and people around the world are already aware of its quality. We plan on leveraging the Tasty Singapore brand to enhance our brand and build selective partnerships. There are many companies who compete in this area but our customers can easily recognise and appreciate superior quality."

Tai Hua Food Industries Pte Ltd
12 Jalan Besut
Singapore 919566
+ 65 6265 9911 tel
+ 65 6265 4077 fax
taihua@singnet.com.sg
www.taihua.biz
Registered brands: KING, Tai Hua

Tat Hui Foods
The Noodle Revolution

Tat Hui Foods has taken the instant noodle phenomenon to a new level of health and variety. Through extensive R&D, Tat Hui has perfected the art of producing steam-cooked noodles that are air-dried and never fried, removing the fat content found in most instant noodles. With the use of natural ingredients, the company has recreated the delicious taste synonymous with Tat Hui products.

This innovation made Tat Hui the first to produce instant noodles without any added MSG, and also the first to receive the Singapore Health Promotion Board's 'Healthier Choice' endorsement in this category. Its noodle range, which includes the popular Koka, Sanwa and Yoodles brands, contains less than 1% of fat content as compared to the average 20% found in other noodle brands.

The company's tagline "Join the Revolution" emphasises the shift towards healthier eating in its target markets. With more than 90% of its products exported to Europe, Australia, Asia and the Middle East, Tat Hui has customised its noodles to suit the taste palates of each region. Tat Hui's employment of the latest technology and automation ensures high quality standards, fast and smooth food processing and constant innovative development.

"We are always innovating in our products," says Ms Lim Shiang, Marketing Director for Tat Hui Foods. "We want to ensure that our customers are always spoilt for choice when it comes to their selection of tasty yet healthy instant noodles, while maintaining a high level of environmental consciousness. With the Tasty Singapore endorsement, we plan to bring that level of quality to various emerging markets."

Tat Hui Foods Pte Ltd
37 Quality Road
Singapore 618808
+ 65 6261 1010 tel
+ 65 6265 1929 fax
thf@pacific.net.sg
www.tathui.com
Tasty Singapore-endorsed brands: KOKA

Tee Yih Jia Food Manufacturing
Pastry to be Reckoned With

With a history of more than 30 years, a string of awards and accolades, Tee Yih Jia Food Manufacturing enjoys meteoric success in more than 50 countries. Today, the company's key objective is to build strategic alliances with reputable global partners and establish an Asian food consortium of food and beverage companies in the region to enjoy multiple cross-synergies.

This push to improve vertical integration, expand marketing channels and enhance collective economies of scale has allowed the company to stay on the cutting edge of product innovation and application, manufacturing quality, automation and market penetration. It has achieved and sustained strong penetration in its key markets of Asia, Europe and the USA. With manufacturing facilities in Singapore, China, Malaysia and the USA, coupled with an extensive global network of distributors, Tee Yih Jia's products are marketed to most parts of the world. Today, more than 90% of Tee Yih Jia's turnover is contributed by the overseas markets.

"Timing plays a pivotal role in determining the success of our business," says Mr Sam Goi, Executive Chairman of Tee Yih Jia. "Besides being at the right place, doing the right thing, we must also have the right people to execute our business strategies. The tenets of our success are two-fold: to improve upon yesterday's success; and to continually innovate to ensure tomorrow's success."

Tee Yih Jia's participation in the Tasty Singapore brand is aligned with its drive for a collective consortium in creating multiple synergies and enhancing its marketing channels into emerging markets. Singapore is recognised as an international F&B hub and governed by high production and processing standards, Tee Yih Jia is confident it will reap the benefits of the collective brand.

Tee Yih Jia Food Manufacturing Pte Ltd
1 Senoko Road
Singapore 758134
+ 65 6880 9888 tel
+ 65 6286 2222 fax
tyj@tyjfood.com
www.teeyihjia.com
Tasty Singapore-endorsed brands: HAPPY BELLY, Spring Home

Thong Siek Food Industry
Seafood Delicacies to Whet the Appetite

Thong Siek's commitment to providing healthier food choices for their health-conscious customers is evident in their popular Surimi-based products and strict health and safety production guidelines. Using a healthy recipe of minced fish that is low in cholesterol, fats, calories, salt and sugar, their 'DoDo' brand of products also contain no preservatives and no added MSG for a healthy, balanced meal solution.

The company's impressive range of Surimi seafood products includes fish balls, breaded fish fingers, crab-flavoured sticks, Thai tom yum fish cakes, and a revolutionary range of convenient seafood meals. Comprising local noodle soup favourites like Laksa Bee Hoon (Coconut Curry Rice Sticks with Fish Cakes), and Fish Ball Soup with Kway Tiao (rice noodles), this range of products comes complete with fresh ingredients, and offers authentic Singapore-style hawker fare in convenient, attractive packaging.

The first seafood company in Southeast Asia to install a fully automated fish ball and fish cake processing line, Thong Siek firmly believes in leveraging technology to improve its processes.

Besides supplying its products to local wet markets, supermarket chains and food outlets, Thong Siek also distributes its products to more than 20 countries worldwide, including Australia, New Zealand, USA, Europe and Asia. In exploring new opportunities in Europe and the Middle East, the country is seeking distributors to help promote the 'DoDo' brand and its products.

"Singapore has long offered an attractive proposition for international food buyers because of the emphasis it places on branding and food safety," says Mr Lim Boon Chay, Chairman and Managing Director of Thong Siek. "That is why there has always been stable demand for food manufactured in Singapore. With the introduction of the Tasty Singapore brand, we hope we can now further improve on this demand, especially for companies looking to compete on a global level."

Thong Siek Food Industry Pte Ltd
14 Senoko Way
Singapore 758035
+ 65 6756 0233 tel
+ 65 6754 4030 fax
diana@thongsiek.com
www.thongsiek.com
Tasty Singapore-endorsed brands: DoDo

Tong Garden Food Products
Nuts about Life

Tong Garden, Asia's largest nuts company, attributes its success to the time-honoured traditions of honesty, integrity, hard work and perseverance epitomised by its founder, Ong Tong Guan.

This reputation of trust, built and maintained with their customers and distributors alike, has aided the company's expansion into new markets and tastes since 1963. The guaranteed excellence of product quality stems from its top graded raw materials used to produce its extensive range of products, which comprises its self-titled range of nut products, its 'NOI' brand of Asian Savoury snacks, its youthful 'Craze and Sparkies' brand of uniquely flavoured chips and crackers, and its healthy 'Lite 'n' Natural' range of fruit-and-nut products.

Tong Garden's relentless pursuit of R&D innovation and stringent compliance with Singapore's Good Manufacturing Practices and HACCP guidelines ensures that its products are of high quality standards. Besides local and international retail distribution, Tong Garden also engages in contract manufacturing for private labels.

The company's presence extends to Asia, Australia, New Zealand, Sri Lanka, Bangladesh, the Middle East, Africa, the USA and the Pacific Islands. This extensive network enhances the company's reputation as one of the foremost manufacturers of nuts and snacks in the industry today. The company's corporate tagline, "Always A Moment", conveys that when people buy Tong Garden's products, they are not just buying nuts or snacks, but something that completes the moment, whatever or whenever that moment is.

"Tasty Singapore will definitely enhance our international brand awareness campaign," says Ms Ann Ong, Executive Director of Tong Garden. "We are looking to take the Tong Garden brand more extensively into Europe and Latin America, and the collective branding will give us that extra mileage. We are also looking to extend our franchising and OEM arrangements and will benefit from the credibility of the Tasty Singapore brand."

Tong Garden Food Products (Singapore) Pte Ltd
33 Chin Bee Crescent
Singapore 619901
+ 65 6264 4441 tel
+ 65 6265 4441 fax
marketing@tonggarden.com.sg
www.tonggarden.com.sg
Tasty Singapore-endorsed brands: Tong Garden

Unicurd Food
The Power of Soy

While tofu is widely regarded as highly nutritious, it is largely perceived as an oriental product. However, Unicurd has successfully positioned its tofu products within the genre of fusion food, in a wide range of tastes, forms and textures. Today, Unicurd's tofu come in a variety of flavours and are enjoyed beyond the context of oriental cuisine whether as a snack, appetiser, main course or dessert, and especially by its health-conscious customers.

Distributed together with its own range of soy desserts and soymilk, Unicurd's tofu products enjoy wide popularity in Singapore and overseas. Unicurd also produces tofu for private labels, customising its products to suit customers' specifications.

Regular market research helps Unicurd keep up with market and taste trends. With two to three new products every year, Unicurd is set to launch new flavours in its ready-to-eat range of tofu products, including black pepper and tomato pasta. It has also developed a range of cold, tasty and healthy soy desserts, which it expects will hold great appeal for customers around the world. Unicurd is also developing tofu burgers and steaks for its customers in the USA and Europe. R&D has also extended the shelf life of Unicurd's products up to 90 days, making international export easier. Today, Unicurd's products are exported to the USA, the UK, New Zealand and Europe, including Holland, Germany, France, Sweden and Switzerland.

"The quality and nutritional value of our soy products are our highest priorities" says Mr Francis Goh, Managing Director of Unicurd. "As the first SME in Singapore to receive ISO9001 and HACCP certifications, our manufacturing processes produce the highest quality tofu without compromising on nutritional value."

Unicurd is looking forward to bringing its products as part of the collective Tasty Singapore branding effort to reach new and emerging markets such as the Middle East.

Unicurd Food Company (Pte) Ltd
18 Senoko South Road
Singapore 758089
+ 65 6759 2855 tel
+ 65 6759 5411 fax
ufc@unicurd.com.sg
www.unicurd.com.sg
Tasty Singapore-endorsed brands: Unicurd

Viz Branz
Where Branding is a Lifestyle

With more than 100 registered brands, 35 trademarks registered in 45 countries and 30 commercially viable products, Viz Branz aptly calls itself a branding company.

Derived from the phrase "Vision in Branding with Zest", Viz Branz carries recognisable favourites like Gold Roast, CappaRoma and Café21, the market leader in 2-in-1 coffees, among others. Its seven production and manufacturing locations in the region also produce a range of instant coffees, cereals and porridge, oats, and snack foods.

Viz Branz was one of the first to introduce nutritious 3-in-1 cereals to China through its Gold Roast brand. Its other export markets include Southeast Asia, Indochina, the Middle East, Eastern Europe, Japan and the USA, all of which are serviced by distributors in both retail and food services channels. The company also provides contract manufacturing for private label clients.

Viz Branz has also ventured into the provision of fully automated beverage machines. Marketed to corporate clients, the machines manage up to 18 different products including teas, coffees and cereals.

"We have gone out of our way to try and understand our customers and their lifestyle requirements to cater to their exact needs," says Mr Tan Kok Hiang, Executive Director of Viz Branz. "We have even customised our packaging to suit certain markets. This careful attention to cultural factors has helped us stay competitive in each market without neglecting the needs of the individual customer."

Viz Branz aims to enhance its long-term brand equity through its association with Tasty Singapore, and leverage on the increased exposure in markets like Australia, Europe and the Middle East.

Viz Branz Limited
14 Woodlands Link
Singapore 738739
+ 65 6756 6033 tel
+ 65 6756 2547 fax
enquiries@vizbranz.com
www.vizbranz.com
Tasty Singapore-endorsed brands: Americafe, BenCafe, Café21, Calsome, CappaRomA, Fresh-Up Lemon Tea Mix and Gold Roast

Conversion Tables A Helpful Guide

Conversion of weight from Metric to Imperial

5 g	1/8 oz	100 g	3 1/2 oz	350 g	12 oz
10 g	1/4 oz	115 g	4 oz	400 g	14 oz
15 g	1/2 oz	125 g	4 1/2 oz	450 g	1 lb
25/30 g	1 oz	140 g	5 oz	500 g	1 lb 2 oz
35 g	1 1/4 oz	150 g	5 1/2 oz	600 g	1 lb 5 oz
40 g	1 1/2 oz	175 g	6 oz	700 g	1 lb 9 oz
50 g	1 3/4 oz	200 g	7 oz	800 g	1 lb 12 oz
55 g	2 oz	225 g	8 oz	900 g	2 lb
60 g	2 1/4 oz	250 g	9 oz	1 kg	2 lb 4 oz
70 g	2 1/2 oz	275 g	9 3/4 oz	1.5 kg	3 lb 5 oz
85 g	3 oz	280 g	10 oz	1.8 kg	4 lb
90 g	3 1/4 oz	300 g	10 1/2 oz	2 kg	4 lb 8 oz
				2.25 kg	5 lb

Measuring Cups and Measuring Spoon Sets

Graduated measuring cups are made in 1/4 cup, 1/3 cup, 1/2 cup, 1 cup and 2 cup sizes. Measuring spoon sets usually comes in 1/8 teaspoon, 1/4 teaspoon, 1/2 teaspoon, 1 teaspoon and 1 tablespoon volumes. 3 teaspoons make 1 tablespoon. *tsp = teaspoon tbsp = tablespoon.*

TABLESPOONS	CUPS	FLUID OUNCES	MILLILITRES	OTHER
1 tablespoon	1/16 cup	1/2 oz	15 ml	
2 tablespoons	1/8 cup	1 oz	30 ml	
		1 1/2 oz	44 ml	1 jigger
4 tablespoons	1/4 cup	2 oz	60 ml	
5 1/3 tablespoons	1/3 cup	2 1/2 oz	75 ml	
8 tablespoons	1/2 cup	4 oz	125 ml	1/4 pint
10 2/3 tablespoons	2/3 cup	5 oz	150 ml	
12 tablespoons	3/4 cup	6 oz	175 ml	
16 tablespoons	1 cup	8 oz	237 ml	1/2 pint
	4 cups	32 oz	946 ml	1 quart or 1 liter
	8 cups	64 oz		2 quarts
	16 cups	128 oz		1 gallon

Oven Temperatures
An approximate conversion chart

CELSIUS	FAHRENHEIT	GAS MARK	DESCRIPTION
105 C	225 F	1/4	Very cool
120 C	250 F	1/2	Very cool
130 C	275 F	1	Cool
150 C	300 F	2	Cool
165 C	325 F	3	Very moderate
180 C	350 F	4	Moderate
190 C	375 F	5	Moderate
200 C	400 F	6	Moderately hot
220 C	425 F	7	Hot
230 C	450 F	8	Hot
245 C	475 F	9	Very hot

Recipe Index

International Enterprise Singapore

International Enterprise (IE) Singapore is an agency under the Ministry of Trade and Industry spearheading the development of Singapore's external economy.

Our mission is to promote overseas growth of Singapore-based enterprises and international trade. With a global network in over 30 locations and our '3C' framework of assistance – Connections, Competency, Capital, we offer products and services to help enterprises export, develop business capabilities, find overseas partners and enter new markets.

At the same time, we work to position Singapore as a base for foreign businesses to expand into the region in partnership with Singapore-based enterprises. Singapore's unique advantages of strategic location, stable government, competitive workforce, and pro-business environment make it an ideal launch pad for globalisation.

IE Singapore assists enterprises across a wide range of industries with focus on eight key clusters: Business Services, Electronics & Precision Engineering, Infocomm Technology, Infrastructure Services, Environmental Services, International Trading, Lifestyle and Transport & Logistics.

Products and Services

Competency

IE Singapore has a wide range of assistance programmes and resources to help Singapore-based enterprises build internationalisation competencies. Our capability development programmes, publications, trade statistics and online portal (www.iesingapore.com) provides enterprises with the assistance and information to develop their business capabilities in some of the following – branding, design, manpower, distribution, intellectual property and financial management amongst others.

Connections

IE Singapore's global network offers businesses the necessary connections to venture overseas. Whether you are looking for suppliers or joint venture partners in Singapore or overseas, our online business matching services such as Buy Singapore (www.buysingapore.com), business networking platforms and business missions to overseas markets can provide the right channels to get you connected.

Capital

To help enterprises gain access to capital, develop their financial management capabilities and to defray developmental costs of expanding overseas, IE Singapore provides a series of financial tools, grants and tax incentives to help companies explore overseas business opportunities confidently.

Please visit www.iesingapore.com for more information. For enquiries, please contact our Customer Service Centre at 1800-IESPORE (local toll-free), +65 63376628 or write to us at www.iesingapore.com/contactus.

For more information,
please visit **www.iesingapore.com**

International Enterprise Singapore
230 Victoria Street #09-00
Bugis Junction Office Tower
Singapore 188024
+65 6337 6628 tel
+65 6337 6898 fax

Promoting overseas growth and international trade
Bangkok • Beijing • Chengdu • Chennai • Chongqing • Dalian • Doha • Dubai • Frankfurt • Guangzhou • Hanoi • Ho Chi Minh City • Hong Kong • Jakarta • Kuala Lumpur • London • Los Angeles • Mexico City • Moscow • Mumbai • New Delhi • New York • Qingdao • Santiago • Sao Paulo • Seoul • Shanghai • Singapore • Stockholm • Sydney • Taipei • Tokyo • Xi'an

Notes

Notes

July 2007

Written by Violet Oon

Writing on Tasty Singapore and Brand Ambassadors as well as editing by The Writer's Ring

Designed and produced by SiliconPlus Communications Pte Ltd

Published by
International Enterprise Singapore
230 Victoria Street #09-00
Bugis Junction Office Tower
Singapore 188024

1800-IESPORE (1800-4377673) local toll-free
+ 65 6337 6628 tel
+ 65 6337 6898 fax
www.iesingapore.com
www.tastysingapore.com

Second Edition 2007

Printed and bound in Singapore

ISBN-10: 981-05-7826-1